ISLAND DREAMS
CARIBBEAN

Joan Tapper   Photographs by Nik Wheeler

ISLAND DREAMS
CARIBBEAN

With 256 color illustrations

Thames & Hudson

CONTENTS

First published in 2005 in hardcover
in the United States of America by
Thames & Hudson Inc., 500 Fifth Avenue,
New York, New York 10110

thamesandhudsonusa.com

Library of Congress Catalog Card Number
2004195111

ISBN-13: 978-0-500-51236-4
ISBN-10: 0-500-51236-1

Printed and bound in China by Toppan

Page 1 On Mullet Bay Beach, St. Martin.

Frontispiece Paradise Beach,
Carriacou, Grenada.

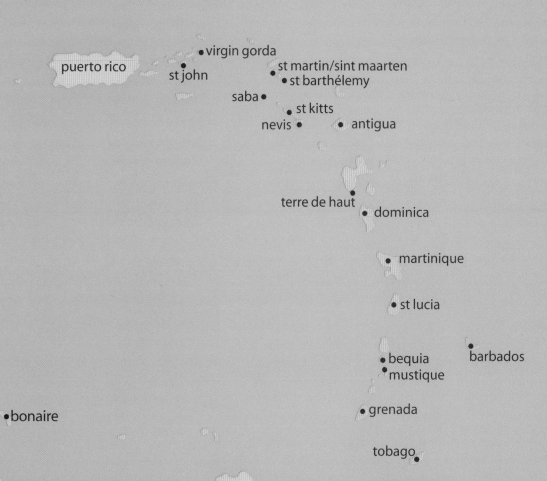

caicos

turks

dominican
republic

puerto rico

virgin gorda

st john

st martin/sint maarten

st barthélemy

saba

st kitts

nevis

antigua

terre de haut

dominica

martinique

st lucia

bequia

barbados

mustique

curaçao

bonaire

grenada

tobago

VENEZUELA

TRINIDAD

Colonial-style ornamentation survives on the balconies around the church square in Soufrière, original French capital of St. Lucia.

Flamingo pink, the colour of Bonaire's signature bird, adds an inviting glow to a café-bar on Kaya Craane in Kralendijk.

Toes in soft sand. A sip of rum punch and the aroma of nutmeg. The sounds of steel-pan music. A vision of brilliant blue water. Dreams of the Caribbean feed all our senses, in ways as numerous and varied as the islands themselves. This book is a celebration of those islands, the result of a year's worth of journeys, full of unforgettable experiences and generous people.

On a map the isles make a neat little arc around a compact sea, but the uniform look is deceptive; they're hardly all the same. Florida's peninsula points to the four largest islands: Cuba, the Dominican Republic/Haiti, Jamaica and Puerto Rico make up the Greater Antilles; with mountain ranges, miles of beaches, historic sites and secret corners, they are a world of possibilities unto themselves. The Lesser Antilles, curve east and south, like sparkling jewels falling off a table. They may be smaller, but their contrasts still startle. Some, like Martinique, are crowned by towering peaks, whose slopes are blanketed with verdant rain forest. Others, like Curaçao, have a lively capital chock-a-block with architectural treasures. Some islands, like Antigua, boast dozens of glorious beaches. Still others – St. Barts, for instance – have bars, restaurants and discos that are crowded all night. And in some places, like Bonaire, the most memorable scenery is underwater, in coral reefs teeming with colourful marine life.

The islanders may speak English, French, Spanish or Dutch, with a lilting accent or a patois that blends those cultures with a couple of others. Portuguese, Swedes, Danes and Latvians, as well as Amerindian and African tribes, contributed to the languages, traditions and

personalities of the Caribbean islands today. Just before the beginning of Lent, for example, Carnival breaks out with the biggest annual party in the Caribbean, celebrated with masquerades, parades, concerts and a year's worth of zeal. In Curaçao, the festivities also include the island's own music, called *tumba*, a combination of road-march and political commentary sung by musicians who compete to reign as that year's king. A few months later, at the end of July, Barbados has its own version of Carnival, weeks of partying known as Crop Over.

Other holidays pass more quietly. On St. Kitts and Nevis, on Good Friday afternoon, kites rise in the sky, as fathers and sons enact a symbolic resurrection with a tradition passed on for generations. And Christmas on Virgin Gorda, in the British Virgin Islands, calls for the island's own version of yule trees: agave spikes spray-painted silver and hung with glittery ornaments.

Games are yet another kind of local ritual. Football (soccer) matches, horse races, yacht regattas and transatlantic sailboat competitions all bring out islanders to watch, wager and root for their favourites. In places with a British heritage, white-clad cricketers take their places on green country pitches on weekend afternoons. In the Dominican Republic, baseball kindles island passions. But the quirkiest sport may just take place on Tobago, where Easter goat races are a hilarious yearly highlight.

Each island in the Caribbean has its particular story, symbolized in some small way in a hilltop fortress or a town's central square, but the history

At the market in Marigot, capital of French St. Martin, a local fruit and vegetable seller keeps up her pattern of daily life.

The flavours of Creole cuisine depend on fresh exotic spices, like those for sale by the bagful in St. Martin.

of the entire region is a more convoluted saga – a tale of explorers and pirates, of great powers and remote colonies, of gold, sugar and rum. It begins centuries ago with the migration of peoples from South America. Though no one agrees exactly when, long before the fifteenth century a group called the Arawak or Taino settled in the islands. Behind them, also from the south, came the Caribs, a fierce people whose name lives on in the word 'Caribbean'.

The Indians' way of life would change forever after Christopher Columbus sailed into the southern Bahamas on 12 October 1492, with a royal grant from the Spanish monarchs to claim the Indies. He pronounced the islands 'most beautiful' and went on to Cuba and Hispaniola; three more voyages over the next ten years would take the explorer to Jamaica, down the Antilles, and to the South American continent itself. The Spaniards who followed him built a capital on Hispaniola, laying out the historic streets of Santo Domingo's Colonial Zone. They constructed forts and settlements: Havana, Cuba; San Juan, Puerto Rico; and Spanish Town, Jamaica. But they were after more than real estate; it was silver and gold they wanted. Forcing the indigenous Indians to work in their mines, they soon killed off the gentle islanders with hard work and disease. The warlike Caribs, however, resisted the Europeans, fighting, winning a few battles, losing most, and retreating from island to island, until they were chased to mountainous redoubts on Dominica, where some three thousand of their descendants live today. To replace their workers, the Spaniards brought slaves from Africa, chained in the foul bowels of ships. Over the next few centuries the

children and grandchildren of Africans would become the dominant people on almost all of the islands. Their heritage would help shape religion, art, folklore and music throughout the region.

By the seventeenth century, French, British and Dutch privateers (pirates licensed by European powers) all needed bases from which to stage their raids. Though they were not looking for colonies at first, the British soon established settlements in Barbados, Antigua, and Nevis, and they shared St. Kitts with the French, who also put down roots on Martinique and Guadeloupe. The French divided St. Martin with the Dutch, who had trading centres on salt-rich Curaçao and Bonaire. Even Latvians, known as 'Courlanders', got into the act on little Tobago, far to the south. Gradually the Europeans carved the land into plantations and tried growing crops like cotton, indigo, ginger and tobacco. It was sugarcane, however, that really flourished; it would rule the Caribbean's destiny for a long time to come.

Sugar kindled Europe's desire for sweets, and one island after another grew fabulously wealthy on its trade; first Barbados, then Tobago, St. Kitts, Jamaica, western Hispaniola, and later Cuba each prospered in their turn. Where sugarcane would not grow, islanders eked out a living by gathering salt or going out to fish. The dry, low-lying Bahamas, well placed along the sea-lanes, turned into a lair for pirates. By the 1720s, however, piracy was basically a thing of the past. The Spanish had already built their citadels. Now the other European nations showed their might – and protected their prized sugar provinces – with great forts like Brimstone Hill on St. Kitts; Shirley Heights, which guarded the naval

Polynesia comes to St. Barthélemy in the form of a playful surf shop sign across from the beach in Saint-Jean.

Pearly treasures of the Caribbean sea, queen conch shells glisten at a souvenir stand in St. Kitts.

station on Antigua; and Fort Saint-Louis in Martinique. Those bastions were a reflection of the times, as the continental battles between the British and the French were played out in the Caribbean throughout the eighteenth century.

The back-breaking work in the sugarcane fields went on, with slaves planting and harvesting, running the mills and the boiling-houses. Some worked as domestic servants; others became artisans; in the French islands, a mixed-race Creole class arose. But mostly island society was strictly stratified by race. Revolts were common – and cruelly put down. Slavery was finally abolished in the nineteenth century: Britain shut down the slave trade first, then stopped the infamous practice in its colonies in 1838. Over the next decade other islands followed suit, though slavery remained legal in Puerto Rico until 1873 and only ended completely in Cuba in 1886. Without slave labour, the cultivation of sugarcane was no longer so lucrative, though it still affected island events. Sugar politics and military concerns led to the Spanish-American War of 1898, which resulted in Cuban independence. The war also involved the United States in other island affairs; the new superpower took control of Puerto Rico, stepped into Haiti and the Dominican Republic, and acquired three of the Virgin Islands.

In the twentieth century, as Caribbean islands grappled with hard economic times, they increasingly resented colonial rule. In many places local leaders pushed for autonomy, leading a struggle that bore fruit in the 1960s, 1970s and 1980s, as most British islands became independent countries. The French islands remained integral *départements* of France,

however, and the Dutch islands now have an affiliated status with the Kingdom of the Netherlands.

More and more now, it is tourism that charts the course for the Caribbean islands. Today's invaders are hotel guests searching for tropical warmth and exotic scenery. In the process they also encounter a vibrant, multifaceted Caribbean culture with distinctive religions, interesting cuisines, and stories of the island experience illuminated by poets like Aimé Césaire and Nobel Prize laureate Derek Walcott. And always there is music – hip-shaking, soul-stirring, got-to-move music. Calypso, with its roots in Carnival traditions, combines ribald humour and sharp social commentary in catchy popular songs. The oil industry on Trinidad gave birth to steel-pan bands, as surplus oil drums were hammered and tuned to a new, unmistakable Caribbean sound. The Dominican Republic produced *merengue*, Martinique the *beguine*. Cuba's *son* music – just one of its rhythmic dances – became the basis of what is often called *salsa*, and Jamaica's *reggae* has become a major force in the pop music charts. Give in, Caribbean music seems to tell us. Let go. Be seduced by the sun and the sea and the inimitable spirit of the place.

When it came to choosing the islands to include here, we faced some hard decisions. We looked for appealing natural land- and seascapes as well as man-made charm, and we tried to mix off-the-beaten-path discoveries with places that travellers had loved for years. We wanted to represent English, French, Spanish, Dutch and U.S. islands. And though

Carib designs etched and repainted on a rock face commemorate the scene of a dreadful massacre at Bloody Point on St. Kitts.

One wears shoes, the other doesn't in rural Sánchez, a gateway to the Dominican Republic's Samaná Peninsula.

the Bahamas Out Islands and the Turks and Caicos Islands are technically in the Atlantic, they are bound to the Caribbean by history and culture, and so each of them has a chapter here.

How to group them? Geographic divisions made little sense; neighbouring islands might have little in common – not language, customs, nor terrain. We settled instead on four sections that broadly reflect what a visitor might experience.

Antigua, Barbados, Curaçao, Martinique, St. Barts, and St. Martin/Sint Maarten make up 'Sophisticated Getaways'. Though these islands have well-developed tourism and are crisscrossed by networks of roads, they are not all alike. Some emphasize heritage and history; others pursue the latest trend. Some have smart shops, others elegant restaurants; there are a few classic resorts on some of these islands, on others visitors stay in villas and venture out to casinos and discos for entertainment.

'Quiet Gems' includes the Bahamas Out Islands, Grenada, the Grenadines, Nevis, St. Kitts, St. Lucia, Terre de Haut, and Tobago. These islands vary greatly in size and landscape from mountainous Grenada to flat Bahamian cays. The bigger places may have towns and harbours, or even hotel enclaves with marinas, restaurants and late-night bars, but they often share the island with silent forests or traditional fishing villages and wild country roads. As for the smaller isles, they are sweet spots to get away from it all.

'Adventurers' Delights' welcome visitors with outdoor passions and a commitment to the land and sea environment. Bonaire, Dominica, Saba, St. John, Turks and Caicos, and Virgin Gorda are superb pleasure grounds

for pursuits like sailing, snorkelling and diving, fishing and hiking. Of course, when the day's activity is over, there are fine places to stay in as well.

The last part highlights Cuba, the Dominican Republic, Jamaica and Puerto Rico, islands whose size, topography, and internal variety offer 'Something for Everyone' (even Americans who, although they are officially forbidden to travel to Cuba and 'trade with the enemy', frequently find their way there through third countries). These islands are big, impossible to drive around in a day or even two. They have impressive mountain ranges, lovely beaches and quiet villages, as well as the region's most historic cities – Old Havana, Santo Domingo's Colonial Zone, and Old San Juan. The islands have their share of music and night-life, opportunities to hike, dive and fish, challenging golf-courses and equestrian trails, as well as resorts with all kinds of sports facilities and guest-houses where the best choice is to do absolutely nothing at all.

We recognize that these generalizations will last only a moment. The islands change with every season. New hotels come and go, along with spas and restaurants. Once-tiny crossroads towns grow into sprawling resorts. And even now the categories cannot be cast in stone. You can savour quiet moments in sophisticated getaways and check into famed hideaways on the tiniest tranquil isle. As for adventure . . . well, many travellers will find a way to create their own. And in the end, that really is what this book is about. Island dreams can be quietly seductive – a nap in a hammock, a whisper of romance and a sip of fine rum. But island dreams are even better as inspiration, when they invite you to sail away and embrace the reality for yourself.

sophisticated getaways

antigua

barbados

curaçao

martinique

st barthélemy

st martin/sint maarten

Sherbet colours enliven the Dutch-style façades that front St. Anna's Bay in Curaçao's capital, Willemstad, thanks to a colonial governor who said the town's traditional white architecture hurt his eyes. Today, shops and cafés thrive in a World Heritage Site filled with renovated buildings.

antigua

The Sunday afternoon jump-up at Shirley Heights creates a scene that blends Antigua's past and present. Here, at a bluff-top fortification more than two hundred years old, tourists gyrate to a steel-pan band as chefs tend barbecued ribs and chicken. The visitors down rum punch and Wadadli beer and toast the sun as it sinks behind English Harbour.

The largest of the Leeward Islands – a hilly 108 square miles – was home to Amerindians before Columbus named it Santa Maria de la Antigua in 1493. A lack of fresh water discouraged the Spanish but not the British, who claimed the island in 1627 and made it their biggest naval station after Jamaica. Unlike most Caribbean isles, which were traded among the European powers, Antigua remained almost continually British until independence, which came in 1981 and included quiet neighbour Barbuda.

Roads radiate across the island through quiet villages to isolated peninsulas and myriad coves and bays. In the east, one track leads to Devil's Bay, where explosive waves carve the limestone tableland. Curving Fig Tree Drive leads south over volcanic mountains lush with bananas (known here as figs), yams, dasheen, guavas and pineapple. The gorgeous sandy beaches, 365 in all, locals claim, have been luring tourists for decades. In the north, Dickenson and Runaway Bays are lined with hotels. Long Bay, on the eastern coast, lives up to its name; and Half Moon Bay is a wild, wave-washed crescent. Hawskbill Bay is a pretty strand at Five Islands, west of St. John's, the capital.

The island's main town boasts an intriguing smattering of antique architecture. At the top of Temple Street stands the stately Anglican cathedral of St. John's, rebuilt in 1847 with ornate twin towers and a wooden interior. Near the dock, the centuries-old warehouses of Redcliffe Quay have been brightly painted and reborn as shops, cafés, bars and restaurants. And the neoclassical freestone court-house, erected in 1750, now houses the Museum of Antigua and Barbuda. Exhibits range from natural history, slavery and sugarcane – the main crop on the island until 1960 – to contemporary sports: the record-breaking bat and ball used by native son Viv 'Master Blaster' Richards attests to the national passion for cricket.

More of the sugar story is explained at Betty's Hope Plantation, which dates from 1650. Though the manor house is gone, twin mills still stand. About a decade ago the community united to restore one windmill and rehang its sails, turning a relic into a working testament to generations of islanders who toiled in the cane fields, harvested the crop and processed the sugar. Living history also has a showcase at English Harbour, a natural hurricane hole that grew into an important eighteenth-century dockyard, named for Horatio Nelson, who served here as a captain. In its heyday huge wheel-shaped capstans pulled ships over on their side for careening, but the port closed in 1889. In the mid-twentieth century the Georgian buildings were restored as a museum, hotel, restaurants and vital ships' stores to become a national park. Neighbouring Falmouth Harbour continues the seafaring tradition with a thriving marina that comes to boisterous life every April with Sailing Week, a world-class regatta with world-class parties. For the rest of the year, there's Sunday at Shirley Heights.

A riffle of foam washes up on the beach at Curtain Bluff Resort (*opposite*), on the south coast of Antigua. This area, near Cades Reef, offers terrific snorkelling, but with hundreds of coves for a visitor to choose from, there's a sandy stretch for every mood. Johnson's Point (*above*), a bit farther west, provides shelters from the Caribbean sun, a ruined fort to explore, and a view toward Montserrat.

Namesake saints, statues taken from a French ship, guard the entrance to the Anglican cathedral of St. John's (*below*), rebuilt in 1847 after an earthquake destroyed an earlier stone church in the capital. Islanders encased the interior in pine, hoping to avoid future devastation. Only evocative pillars are left from the boat-house (*opposite*) in Nelson's Dockyard, which re-creates the Georgian naval yard where Horatio Nelson served early in his career. The garden at water's edge is part of the Admiral's Inn, located in a centuries-old engineer's office and warehouse.

Market Street flows north and south through the centre of St. John's (*opposite*), where islanders come to shop and conduct their business, and where a street preacher tries to convert passers-by (*left*). The town dates from the late 1700s and has its share of historic buildings in Georgian, Romantic and vernacular styles. Heritage Quay is a modern innovation, welcoming cruise-ship visitors with the sounds of a steel-pan band (*above*).

antigua **sophisticated getaways**

19

The Shirley Heights panorama (*above*) overlooks the sinuous indentations of a natural hurricane hole. Nelson's Dockyard shelters dozens of sailboats; just beyond, English Harbour's marinas provide berths for countless other vessels. Every year these south-coast anchorages welcome competitive sailboats to the rowdy sea-going party called Antigua Sailing Week. But on any given day Curtain Bluff beach invites island dreamers to sail off into the sunset (*opposite*).

barbados

In feathers, sequins and skin-hugging spandex, the costumed paraders 'jumped' their way into the stadium and then out through the streets of Bridgetown. More than 10,000 revellers, organized into themed bands, were taking part in the Grand Kadooment. After weeks of calypso competitions, all-night parades and band exhibitions with colourful names like Cohobblopot, this was the culmination of Crop Over, Barbados's annual carnival. It commemorates the plantation owners' custom of allowing a day for celebration after the sugarcane crop was in.

Heritage and tradition – from festivals to architectural treasures to a national enthusiasm for cricket – are important on Barbados, which probably got its name from Portuguese explorers in the 1500s, who called it Los Barbados after the bearded fig trees. The British then happened on the island, which lies to the east of the main Caribbean chain, in 1625. They built the first settlement at Holetown two years later, starting a rare, unbroken period of rule that ended only with independence in 1966. By the mid-1600s sugar had been planted, and African slaves were brought to work the crop. It made the island wealthy and led to the establishment of cities and institutions that remain to this day: the capital of Bridgetown (1628), Barbados's own parliament (1639), the Bridgetown Synagogue (1654), St. Michael's Anglican Cathedral (1665) and a noted rum industry.

Over the next two centuries, Barbados grew into a prominent colony, one of three main points – with London and Boston – of the British Empire. Bridgetown became an important careenage for refurbishing ships; it remains a major cruise-ship port. And redbrick Georgian military buildings went up around the Garrison Savannah parade ground, today a race-track and favourite jogging path. At a house nearby, being renovated as a museum, a young George Washington spent six weeks, the only place where the future President of the United States ever lived abroad.

Around the island other great houses and historical sites have also been preserved: the Morgan Lewis Sugar Mill, for instance, demonstrates how the cane was ground. St. Nicholas Abbey (a Jacobean-style house), Francia Plantation, Sunbury House and the Tyrol Cot complex showcase the furnishings and lifestyle of earlier ages. In contrast are the chattel houses – those tiny, colourful, gingerbread-trimmed cottages that were built to be disassembled and moved. They are visible along the meandering byways that connect Barbados's villages and pass its fields of sugarcane, still the main crop.

Underneath the soil is an island of limestone, roughly 14 by 21 miles. The hilly centre has botanical gardens and underground caverns. In the north and east, rugged hills are reminiscent of the Highlands, accounting for the nickname, 'the Scotland District'. On the Atlantic coast, at Bathsheba,

East Side story: great boulders dominate the Atlantic coast around Bathsheba (*opposite*), where the currents discourage casual swimmers but the waves attract world-class surfers in winter. Summer's highlight in Barbados is the Crop Over festival; one member of a marching troupe (*above*) has a smile that outshines her glitter.

giant boulders are washed by crashing waves that attract champion surfers. Casual bathers head to the white-sand strands of the south – Bottom Bay, Crane Beach, Dover and Casuarina Beaches – where guest-houses, restaurants and nightspots have sprung up to cater for ever-increasing numbers of visitors from Britain and North America. Extending north from Bridgetown, in the south-western corner, the 'platinum' coast has also been developed with a string of luxurious villas, spectacular hotels, fine dining spots and golf-courses.

Yet sophisticated, contemporary Barbados has not given up its traditions. At Speightstown, guides lead visitors on the Arbib Trail, which crosses wild gullies and wanders through the town, where islanders share their folkways and their living Bajan heritage.

The sunset at Holetown (*below*) – where the first European settlers arrived in 1627 – brings out locals for a beer.

More elegant libations have a place at Villa Nova (*left and top*), built in 1834 and once owned by British Prime Minister Sir Anthony Eden; today the former plantation house has been turned into a country hotel. Historic portraits underline the heritage of St. Nicholas Abbey (*above*), another Great House and one of the oldest residences on the island, from 1660.

Bay Street (*opposite*), one of the main thoroughfares of Bridgetown, runs to
the capital's inner harbour, once an important careenage for sailing ships,
and across to the heart of the city, a centre of commerce since the mid-1600s.
In Holetown (*above*), a restaurant's up-to-date graphics draw attention to its
welcoming attitude.

Overleaf Crop Over is Carnival Barbados-style, an unbridled island-wide fête at the traditional end of the sugarcane harvest in late July and August. Days of parades, concerts and musical competitions come to a gala finale with thousands of costumed revellers marching behind bands through the sports stadium and into the streets.

curaçao

The townhouses that flank Willemstad's St. Anna's Bay have the flat façades, neat curving gables and window details you would expect of any city in the Netherlands. But, oh, those tropical colours – butterscotch, robin's egg blue, cotton candy pink! The Caribbean palette has left its distinctive mark on the colonial architecture of Curaçao in the Netherlands Antilles, which was named a World Heritage Site in 1997.

Though the Spanish settled here in 1499 and the British ruled briefly twice, the Dutch have generally held sway on the island since they took possession in 1634. They liked its deep, hidden harbour and the salt lakes that dotted its 38-mile length. They fortified St. Anna's Bay and laid out a walled town, which has now become the business district of Punda.

Today, historic and cultural sites abound, with more than 5,000 listed buildings. The garrison of Fort Amsterdam has become the centre of island administration. (The Netherlands Antilles have had self-government within the Dutch kingdom since 1955.) The Fort Church, built in 1769, has ceilings high enough to dry sails beneath them, and the nearby Postal Museum occupies a family house constructed in the1690s. Jewish traders were among Curaçao's first colonists; in 1732 they built Mikvé Israel-Emanuel, the oldest synagogue still in continuous operation in the Western Hemisphere, with a mahogany dais, elaborate candlelit chandeliers and a floor of sand.

In the Floating Market at the edge of Punda, schooners selling produce from Venezuela, just 35 miles away, tie up behind stalls piled high with hot peppers, spices, cheeses and fish, while the sounds of Papiamento – the local tongue drawn from the Dutch, Spanish, English, Portuguese, African and Amerindian languages – fill the air. The Queen Emma pontoon bridge crosses the bay to the lively residential area called Otrobanda. On the site of long-ago slave auctions a new museum commemorates the cultures of West Africa and the history of the slave trade. And for blocks around, barbershops and hairdressers jostle for space with the eighteenth- and nineteenth-century mansions and cottages that are benefiting from the city's vibrant preservation movement.

Out in the *kunuku*, or countryside, the pace slows. A hundred plantations once divided the arid, cactus-filled landscape. Their ochre-walled *landhuises*, colonial houses, are still noticeable on hilltops; Knip was the site of a notorious slave rebellion in 1795. Carefully restored Groot Santa Martha houses a sheltered workshop. Jan Kock contains an art gallery, Chobolobo is home to the Curaçao liqueur factory and Daniel has been transformed into a restaurant and guest-house.

Coral-sand beaches for swimming, snorkelling and diving scallop the serene southern coast – Barbara Beach, Playa Porto Marie, Cas Abou, and Playa Knip, among them – all the way to Westpunt. Inland, Mount Christoffel, at 1,237 feet, dominates Christoffel National Park. Jeep and

Venezuelan boats selling fish, fruits and vegetables create the Floating Market (*opposite*) along the waterfront in Willemstad. The vendors tie up for several days at a time, then return to South America, about 35 miles away, to replenish their stock. Stretching back from the water is Punda, the shopping district that follows the grid of the colonial Dutch city, laid out in the seventeenth century. Jewish families were among Curaçao's earliest settlers; they built the Mikvé Israel-Emanuel synagogue (*above*), with its unusual sand floor and candlelit chandeliers, in 1732.

hiking trails offer glimpses of parrots and troupials, blue-green iguanas and, occasionally, Curaçao deer, as well as views to the sea. The park also encompasses Shete Boka, on the rugged northern coast, where surf crashes on the limestone tableland with a wild fury that seems miles away from sophisticated Willemstad.

Crosses reach to the blue heavens from gleaming graves at a country cemetery in San Willibrordo (*opposite*), up the coast from the capital. Jewish merchants built the Italianate nineteenth-century mansions in the Scharloo neighbourhood of Willemstad. Among the best known is the beautifully preserved Wedding Cake House (*below*), with its ornamental icing.

Overleaf Waves shoot skyward at Boka Tabla as they crash into the limestone tablelands on the wild northern shore, part of Shete Boka National Park, which protects several blowholes, a cave, a natural bridge and a sea turtle sanctuary. The other coast of the island is far more placid, with a series of beaches that extend from the fishermen's settlement at Westpunt (*top right*) to the sandy stretch at Playa Porto Marie (*centre right*) and at Playa Abou (*bottom right*).

Columns and arches in tutti-frutti shades are a hallmark of Punda's architecture (*left*). The patterns are more angular in the modern housing just across the inlet (*opposite*). Not far away, two women in Curaçao's national costume watch the passing scene from the entry of an arts and cultural centre (*above*).

martinique

The exquisite Balata Garden, on the squiggly road to Martinique's rain-forest interior, is awash in colours and textures: pink and red gingers, brilliant anthurium and pendulous heliconia are interspersed with spiky bromeliads and an array of begonia. It is easy to see why the indigenous Caribs called their home Madinina, 'island of flowers'. From here, the views take in the varied topography, from the cloud-wreathed Pitons du Carbet in the north, to the bay around Fort-de-France, the sophisticated capital of this overseas *département* of France.

Columbus sighted Martinique in 1493 but never landed till 1502. Instead, it was the French who established the first European settlement, at Saint-Pierre, on the mountainous north-west coast, in 1635. The town grew into a prosperous commercial centre as sugarcane, coffee and cocoa plantations, worked by African slaves, flourished in the fertile volcanic soil. The elegant lifestyle of the planters and the story of those crops, including the distillation of rum, is brought to life in several museums and surviving estates that preserve the atmosphere of bygone centuries. In the late 1600s another city grew up around Fort Saint-Louis, whose stone ramparts were completed in 1703. Fort-de-France blossomed, then became the scene of frequent strife and civil unrest as first the French and the British, then the Royalists and Republicans, battled for supremacy on the island. In the process, slavery was abolished in 1794, but Napoleon later reinstated it, urged on by his Empress Josephine, who had grown up on a Martinique plantation. Only in 1848 was the brutal practice finally stopped for good. Those who championed the cause are remembered on the walls of the landmark Schoelcher Library, an Egyptian-Roman-Byzantine architectural fantasy named after a famed abolitionist.

In May 1902 disaster struck the island: Mount Pelée erupted, killing all 30,000 inhabitants of Saint-Pierre – except for a single soul, who had spent the night in an underground jail. The ruins of shops and houses and a volcanological museum testify poignantly to the destruction.

Still, Martinique's vitality continued to express itself in art, music and poetry. Its Creole sensuality attracted painter Paul Gauguin, and island dances like the *beguine* captivated a wide audience. More recently the catchy beat of *zouk* has made its mark on the world music scene. And poet Aimé Césaire, later the longtime mayor of Fort-de-France, gave voice to the Négritude movement, which embraced African and Caribbean themes.

Today, modern highways branch across and around Martinique's 48- by-19-mile fishhook shape. Everywhere there are reminders of the African, Creole and European cultures that have shaped its identity. Curries and peppers, ginger and nutmeg flavour meat, fish and vegetables; fine rums (distilled here since 1650) and imported wines accompany the cuisine. Village churches resemble small European cathedrals, and shops

The modern town of Saint-Pierre (*opposite*) hugs a black-sand beach on Martinique's north-west coast. The island's original capital, it was a bustling commercial centre until the eruption of Mount Pelée wiped out the city and its inhabitants in May 1902. Rain-forested mountains dominate the interior. The Pitons du Carbet loom almost 4,000 feet high, dwarfing the domed Sacré-Cœur of Balata (*above*), which was constructed in 1923 as a diminutive version of the famous Paris basilica.

Overleaf Though Mount Pelée's ridged summit appears deceptively serene today, evidence of its destructive history is housed in a volcanological museum in Saint-Pierre.

have solid northern façades as often as they are embellished with Antillean gingerbread.

Once quiet fishing villages like Les Anses d'Arlets, Sainte-Luce and Le Marin now include holiday guest-houses or harbours for sleek yachts. Les Trois-Ilets is an established resort, while upscale villas dot the rolling countryside near Le François, where visitors splash offshore in the aqueous blue playground known as Josephine's Bathtub. At weekends everyone throngs the beaches. At Sainte-Anne open-air restaurants serve grilled fish and lobster, and on the white sands of Grande Anse des Salines families hang hammocks in the sea-grape trees and swim and picnic with Martiniquan flair.

The Caribs' name for Martinique, Madinina, meant 'island of flowers'. That horticultural tradition continues at Balata Garden, where a hummingbird prefers its feeder to the blushing orchid, ginger and proteus blooms (*clockwise from top*).

Spices, handicrafts and home-bottled remedies fill the tables at the central market in Fort-de-France (*left*). The island's Creole dishes deliciously blend tropical flavours and ingredients, but fine French cuisine is also prevalent, like this elegant seafood gratin (*above*) at Cap Est Lagoon Resort. In the fishing village of Les Anses d'Arlets (*opposite*), wooden balconies and shuttered façades appear gilded at sunset.

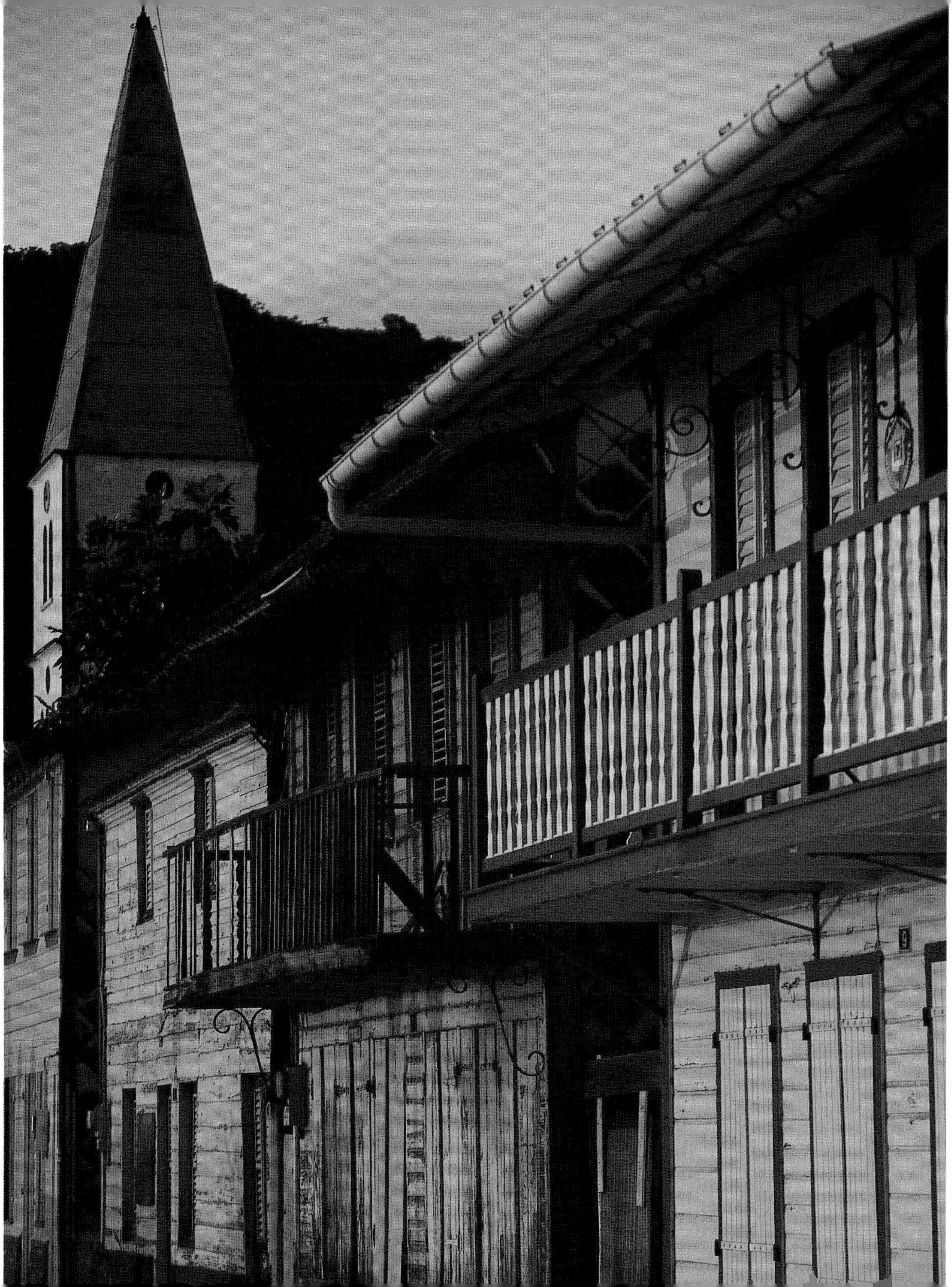

Pleasure boats anchor in the placid waters off Pointe du Bout, across the Bay of Fort-de-France (*opposite*) from the busy capital. This southern peninsula is a favourite resort area for French families, who bask in the late afternoon rays on the beach near Les Anses d'Arlets (*above*).

st barthélemy

Très simple, très chic. The tiny, stylish island of St. Barts – more formally, Saint-Barthélemy – is an, oh, so Gallic corner of the Caribbean. The flight in on a small plane (the only kind that can land on the short, heart-in-your-mouth airstrip) sets a tone of exclusivity and sophistication reflected in local architecture, cuisine, shopping and night-life.

There are twenty-two villages on this hilly, 14-square-mile island, but its heart is the capital of Gustavia, where well-manicured streets and alleyways surround a deep, protected port. The yachts moored here have ocean-liner-like proportions, and the pretty shops bear signs like Armani, Hermès and Cartier. By day, the cafés invite travellers to linger over lunch and a glass of wine. At night, the discos resound with Europop into the early morning hours. Yet, despite the celebrities whose presence adds pizzazz, the scene is less about glitz than insouciance. After all, it was an island hangout called Le Select that inspired the Jimmy Buffett song 'Cheeseburger in Paradise'.

In the last twenty-five years St. Barts has become a retreat for upscale travellers who fill its exclusive hotels or stay in an ever-growing number of villas. Before then, however, life was difficult. The island was settled by the French in 1645, but the dry climate never allowed the establishment of plantations – or the importation of slaves. Instead, the islanders, mostly of Breton or Norman descent, lived on commerce and the hard labour of harvesting salt. In 1784, in exchange for certain trade rights, the French ceded the island to Sweden – Scandinavian ties persist to this day – but got it back 104 years later. (Though St. Barts has since been under the *département* of Guadeloupe, that status is about to change to an as-yet unspecified autonomy.) Agriculture is still virtually unknown. All food – from meat and vegetables to paté, cheese and wine – has to be imported.

Circling the two wings of the V-shaped island is a single main road, a narrow roller-coaster trip that affords superb views of Gustavia, placid Caribbean coves and hillside villas with characteristic hip roofs and pastel walls. Side roads lead down to fine white-sand beaches that attract bathers wearing the latest bikinis – or nothing at all. Lively Baie de Saint-Jean has restaurants and cafés, Anse de Lorient and Anse de Grand Cul-de-Sac abound with water-sports enthusiasts. Anse de Grande Saline is quiet and secluded, while Anse du Gouverneur beckons from the bottom of a plunging road. And Anse à Colombier – a luscious strand backed by daunting cliffs – is accessible only by a cactus-lined path or private yacht.

At sundown the action moves to the restaurants. Classic French, spicy Creole, trendy Asian fusion cuisine are all here, in sophisticated settings that range from an old house above the harbour to a smart resort or a beach-front garden. And there's plenty of time to savour the superb meals: the dance-clubs don't get going till midnight!

Traces of a Scandinavian heritage are visible in the Swedish belfry (*opposite*) – a triangular church clock-tower – which rises just above Gustavia's inner harbour. The lovely capital, named after the late-eighteenth-century King Gustavus III, has preserved many buildings from the Swedish era, which lasted just over a century. Modern villas dot the island's hills; the coast is blessed with myriad white-sand beaches, including Anse de Lorient (*above*).

Filmy curtains add a grace note to an informal restaurant in Saint-Jean (*below*), providing a shady spot to while away the hours. On a sunny day, active pursuits – and less energetic ones – also pass the time. On Shell Beach (*opposite left*), just at the edge of Gustavia, beach-goers can forego the sugary sand to laze on a full-size bed.

st barthélemy **sophisticated getaways**

A traditional sailboat (*top*) skims the harbour beneath the ruins of Fort Gustav during a local regatta, while kite-surfers flock to the shallow waters of Anse de Grand Cul-de-Sac (*above*).

Night-life sparkles on an island beloved by the rich and famous, who find plenty of space to park their supersize yachts in Gustavia (*left*). Abundant bar/restaurants serve everything from French cuisine and fine wines to Asian fusion snacks and sophisticated cocktails. L'Entre'Acte (*above*) pulls in diners for pizza along the waterfront. Hip Nikki Beach (*top*) attracts people into the small hours to its beach-side location in Saint-Jean.

st barthélemy **sophisticated getaways**

st martin/sint maarten

A simple obelisk marks the invisible line between St. Martin and Sint Maarten, one side French, the other Dutch. The two countries share this compact slipper-shaped island (with a huge lagoon where the big toe would be) in a cosy arrangement that goes back more than three centuries.

Spanish explorers had the first claim to the island, but they showed little interest in its dry hills and salt-ponds. They left the place to the French, who came in 1629, and the Dutch, who arrived two years later. And though the Spanish briefly returned, the Dutch and French made their division official in 1648 with a treaty based on a fabled foot race that began from the east coast, at Oyster Pond. According to a story with more colour than fact, a Dutch soldier swigged gin as he walked south, a Frenchman sipped only wine on his northern route… and paced off the larger portion of the 37-square-mile isle. Though the island would change hands sixteen times after that, the historic boundaries have held up, with both sides retaining their own personalities, to say nothing of two political administrations, two school systems, two currencies and two telephone systems.

The Dutch side has the international airport and a busy cruise port in the capital of Philipsburg, which fills a strip of land between a large salt-pond and Great Bay. A new promenade runs along the harbour – a terrific place to marvel at the megaships. The town's narrow streets – frequently bursting with shoppers – are chock-a-block with jewelry stores, liquor emporiums and clothing boutiques centred on Wathey Square and its court-house, built in 1793. Beyond the town, Dutch Sint Maarten also boasts a golf-course and lively night-life, particularly near Maho Bay – glittering casinos, raucous dance clubs and musical revues.

The capital of the French side – famous for its cuisine – is Marigot, which has its own postcard-worthy harbour and its own press of traffic. A market with informal eateries and craft stalls occupies one end of the main square, while brasseries and boutiques displaying French prêt-à-porter front the streets. Fort Saint-Louis, built in 1789, looms on a hill above it all. From those ramparts the island is laid out at one's feet, from the masts in Marigot's marina to the lowlands fringing the airport and the lagoon. The tradition of fine food is especially strong in the seaside village of Grand Case. Restaurants line the single street; little grills called *lolos* cluster in a square. And after dark the place is crowded with a parade of visitors choosing where to dine.

For much of the twentieth century islanders scraped to make a living and the population dwindled. But in the last thirty years St. Martin/Sint Maarten has boomed with hotels, villas and time-share condos and become a crossroads for its surrounding isles. Despite the development, the spectacular white-sand beaches and the azure water have remained untouched.

Of the thirty-seven beaches that edge the coast, Orient Bay is the longest strand, with all kinds of water sports (and nudists at the north end). Long Bay is secluded, Simpson Bay surprisingly uncommercial (though it flanks the airport), Cupecoy calmly clothing optional. Oyster Pond is for snorkelling and body-surfing. They and many others extend their invitation in both Dutch and French.

Fort Saint-Louis, in the French capital of Marigot, was built in 1789 as a fortress against English ships; lookouts there today see mostly pleasure vessels (*opposite*). Many visitors come to sail the channels between St. Martin, Anguilla and St. Barts. Others prefer to remain on land, at Orient Bay Beach on the island's east coast (*above*), for example, where the clothing is optional but lively accessories are *de rigueur*.

St. Martin's version of restaurant row is Grand Case, on the French side of the island. Slumbering by day, the town comes alive at nightfall (*right*) as lovers of fine cuisine throng the dozens of eateries.

Menus offer a range from classic French dishes and Creole fare to Asian cooking or seafood, sometimes served with a water view (*left*). Even the sunset from the town pier is worth savouring (*below*).

The ruins of Fort Amsterdam, built in 1631 as the first Dutch fort in the Caribbean, share a peninsula (*above*) with the Divi Resort on the Dutch half of the island. In the hopping cruise port of Philipsburg, the beach bar at the historic Pasanggrahan (*opposite*) is a quiet oasis and a favourite watering hole. Mullet Bay (*right*), one of the island's thirty-seven beaches, offers another opportunity to escape the crowds and contemplate the eye-popping blues of sea and sky.

Marigot spreads out below the panoramic parapets of Fort Saint-Louis (*right*), which take in everything from the market to the marina and the hazy cone of Saba on the horizon. Sunny symbols of the tropics tend to pop up frequently, on the cruise-ship dock in Philipsburg (*top*), for example, and at a nearby restaurant (*above*).

quiet gems

bahamas out islands

grenada

nevis

st kitts

st lucia

terre de haut

the grenadines

tobago

Lithely climbing for coconuts, a St. Lucian scales a palm on the beach near Soufrière. The tree provides food, drink, building materials – and quintessential island photo ops.

bahamas out islands

The name – from the Spanish *baja mar* – means 'shallow seas', and it refers to the eye-popping blue waters that surround the 700-plus Bahamas islands. Nassau, the capital, lies on small, central New Providence, home to three-quarters of the country's 297,000 people. But extending outward from there are the serene Out Islands, a trove of historic villages, sailors' and fishermen's haunts and newly chic resorts.

A southern Bahamian cay – traditionally San Salvador, though Samana Cay also vies for the honour – was Columbus's first New World landfall on 12 October 1492. Within thirty years the gentle indigenous Arawaks who had greeted him were gone, victims of later Spanish explorers. A century later England staked its claim, and in 1648 religious pilgrims from Bermuda founded the first Bahamian settlement on a long, skinny island they named Eleuthera, after the Greek word for freedom.

Soon, the islands attracted pirates like Edward Teach, alias Blackbeard, who menaced treasure-laden galleons bound for Spain. Long after the pirates had been eradicated, ordinary islanders still found their own way to relieve ships of their cargo: 'wreckers' lit beacons and lured the vessels on to the sharp reefs of the uncharted waters.

Except for a blink of Spanish rule, in 1782–83, the Bahamas remained solidly British; after the American Revolution, the islands became a

sanctuary for Loyalists fleeing the newly independent states. Families from New York and the South settled on Harbour Island, off Eleuthera, as well as in Hope Town on Elbow Cay and New Plymouth on Green Turtle Cay. Their pastel New England-style cottages still set the architectural style along the narrow streets and lend themselves to conversion to quaint bed-and-breakfasts and charming boutiques. The fortunes of the Bahamas waxed and waned and waxed again, as islanders prospered by running blockades during the American Civil War and smuggling rum during Prohibition. But in recent years tourism has fuelled the economy of the country, which became an independent Commonwealth member in 1973.

Each Out Island has its own personality. Andros, the largest, is a wild place riddled with lakes and canals. Just fifty miles from Florida, Bimini's game-fishing paradise was made famous by Ernest Hemingway. Yachties favour the turquoise seas around the Exumas, a streamer of cays with secluded beaches and a few luxury hotels. Farther south, the least developed islands attract mostly divers, bone-fishermen and bird-watchers. Pineapple fields and dairy farms once flourished on Eleuthera, but these days, empty white-sand beaches stretch between the island's sleepy close-knit communities. A five-minute water-taxi ride from Eleuthera's north-east corner leads to Harbour Island; this is

Colour is the key on charming Harbour Island, where the steps of the Blue Bar lead to famed Pink Sand Beach (*opposite*), a delicately shaded three-mile expanse. Queen conch shells decorate the restaurant's stair posts, reminders of the tasty gastropod, a culinary standby gathered from the Bahamas' azure waters. The meat is served in myriad imaginative ways, from chowder to a salad cradled in half a papaya (*above*).

a romantic getaway where celebrities mix with tourists who buzz around in golf carts, dawdle in Dunmore Town, and stroll the three miles of aptly named Pink Sand Beach.

Farther north still are the Abacos, a water-lovers' destination with its own scattering of islets. The kerosene-fuelled Hope Town lighthouse, built in 1864, is the candy-striped symbol of Elbow Cay and a favourite subject for visiting artists, who like the nineteenth-century residences. And on Green Turtle Cay, everyday life in picturesque New Plymouth continues its leisurely pace, while shiny yachts and sailboats fill the marinas and the brilliant hues of surrounding waters beckon visitors to ever remoter cays.

A sun-worshippers' haven on Eleuthera's northern tip, Preacher's Cave Beach (*opposite*) recalls the place where religious pilgrims called Eleutheran Adventurers took refuge in 1648, after their ship ran aground on the sharp reefs of Devil's Backbone. Their leader, William Sayle, preached his sermons from a limestone grotto nearby. Farther south on the 110-mile island, the deep-blue Atlantic stirs beneath the craggy limestone overhangs called The Cliffs (*right*). It's easier sailing in the Abacos, where the waters off a Green Turtle Cay beach (*above*) sparkle irresistibly in the sun.

The neat cottages of Hope Town (*left*), on Elbow Cay, date back to the Loyalists who emigrated from the fledgeling United States after the American Revolution. The village's narrow lanes are marked by informal signs (*bottom*). One points to the old Cholera Cemetery, where scores of victims of an 1850 epidemic are buried. Harbour Island (*below*) also has a rich store of colourful New England-style houses from the same era.

Carved pineapples, a traditional symbol of hospitality, decorate the chair
backs at the Dunmore Beach Club's cosy Harbour Island bar *(opposite)*.
Home-baked goodies come with smiling service at Arthur's Bakery *(above)*,
owned by a former Hollywood screenwriter and his Trinidadian wife. Celebrity
connections are commonplace on the island, which blends chic sophistication
with down-home friendliness.

grenada

'Good morning, sweetheart, good morning. Have a look at my spices,' a vendor calls out. Another beckons to her piles of peppers and eggplants. On a Saturday morning the market square in Grenada's capital of St. George's is particularly lively. While stall-owners offer everything from ground provisions – dasheen and yams – to ladies' underwear, hawkers hold out calabashes filled with nutmeg and mace, or strings of ginger and turmeric with other fragrant herbs ('nature's air-fresheners'). There's good reason why this southern Caribbean isle is known as 'the Spice Island'.

Grenada itself (the country includes little Carriacou and Petit Martinique) forms a rough oval with a little tail indented by sandy bays. But the mountainous interior is rumpled with fertile rain forest and etched with curving roads shaded by giant cotton silk trees, making it seem larger than its 12 by 21 miles.

The isle was sighted by Columbus in 1498, but its fierce Carib inhabitants resisted European settlers until the French finally established themselves in 1650. A year later a band of forty Caribs threw themselves from the northern cliffs at Sauteurs ('Leapers') rather than submit to the foreigners. For the next century the French and British traded power here, until the latter won control in 1783. Independence came in 1974, though nine years later a political-party struggle led to the assassination of Prime Minister Maurice Bishop – and intervention by the United States. Today,

calm and goodwill prevail, along with growing prosperity, as Grenadians return from abroad to build houses and retire, and an increasing number of visitors discovers the island's charms.

From the battlements of Fort George, the view of the capital takes in the protected Carenage, busy with cargo boats and water-taxis. Indeed, this is one of the prettiest ports in the Caribbean, with Georgian-era stone buildings and pastel residences rising up the hills. The road up the west coast leads past broad bays to the fishing town of Gouyave, where a traditional nutmeg station gathers, sorts, processes, then ships the spice around the world. Locally a ubiquitous ingredient, nutmeg is added to ice-cream and to balms for aches and pains.

A working nutmeg and cocoa plantation – along with a small historical museum and a restaurant – is open to the public at Belmont Estate, in the north-east. Not far from there is the River Antoine Rum Distillery, which grows its own sugarcane and brews 135-proof liquor in the old-fashioned manner. From the east-coast centre of Grenville, a twisting rain-forest road leads to Grand Etang Forest Reserve, where casual walkers can follow nature trails and intrepid hikers can climb Mount Qua Qua. The south-west peninsula – including the two miles of white-sand Grand Anse beach – is the tourist centre, with an array of large and small hotels and beach-side restaurants.

Grand Anse beach (*opposite*) makes a water-edged playground for local youngsters at sundown. Its two miles of soft white sand play host to sun-worshipping visitors during the day. Inland, Grenada's terrain is creased with fertile mountain slopes that produce, among many other crops, the nutmegs, cloves, cinnamon and ginger that explain the nickname, 'the Spice Island'. At the Gouyave Nutmeg Processing Station (*above*), the apricot-size nutmegs are collected, dried and sorted by hand.

Storm clouds gather over the majestic mountains of Grenada (*above*), feeding the rain forest that blankets much of the northern part of the island. Grand Etang Forest Reserve was established in 1906 to protect Grenada's watershed. Now it is a focal point for the island's ecotourism. The park's hiking paths and nature trails lead to waterfalls, lakes, mountains and viewpoints, like the Beauséjour overlook (*left*), which offers a glimpse of distant sea.

The hilly St. George's is famous for its collection of fine Georgian buildings, including several churches (*above*). The tower of the Roman Catholic cathedral goes back to 1818. Below it, an assortment of nineteenth-century brick buildings surrounds the U-shaped harbour called the Carenage, which bustles with cargo boats and water taxis before opening to St. George's Bay (*right*).

Every day is market day (*above*) in Grenada's capital, but on Saturday morning especially the place teems with shoppers. Stalls of fruits, vegetables, spices and an assortment of other wares spill out from the historic market building under rainbow-hued umbrellas.

A worker at the Gouyave Nutmeg Processing Station separates different grades of mace (*left and above*), a by-product spice derived from the waxy sheath around each nutmeg. Another low-tech factory, the River Antoine Rum Distillery still grows its own sugarcane, which is crushed for juice that is then heated, fermented and distilled. Spent cane husks called *bagasse* (*opposite*) fuel the traditional boiling process that eventually turns out liquor with a 135-proof kick.

nevis

Inside a restored sugar mill, tables have been set with linen and crystal and candles lit for a romantic dinner. Sugar plantations may be long gone on Nevis, but the past has been comfortably incorporated into a contemporary way of life that is reminiscent of a country-house party. This oval isle is the quiet half of a two-island country with St. Kitts, and its 36 square miles are full of historic mills and manor houses that have been converted to restaurants, hotels and art galleries.

Dominating the scene is Mount Nevis, whose forested 3,232-foot peak is famously shrouded by clouds. It was for that snow-like covering (*nieves*) that Columbus named the place in 1493. Local Caribs inhabited the island when the British settled near Cade's Bay, in 1628. But within two decades, the Europeans had driven the Caribs out, begun to plant sugarcane and brought

enslaved Africans to work the plantations. That story is told through a cluster of reconstructed and preserved houses – from a Carib chief's hut to gingerbread-trimmed cottages – at the Nevisian Heritage Village at Fothergill's, the site of the first sugar estate. Eventually, some eighty-five plantations would make the island wealthy. Sugar money helped build the capital, Charlestown, where many nineteenth-century buildings with wood-trimmed galleries face the quiet streets. The Treasury Building has been renovated as the home of the Tourism Authority, and an old cotton ginnery has been converted to a mall. The stone court-house, from 1825, still carries out its legal functions.

At the north end of town, the birthplace of Alexander Hamilton – one of the founders of the American republic – has been rebuilt and turned into the Museum of Nevis History. A sister museum at the south end of Main Street – near an eighteenth-century hot-spring spa – is devoted to the life of Horatio Lord Nelson. Britain's most famous naval hero first arrived in Nevis in 1784 to enforce the unpopular Navigation Acts. On 11 March 1787, he married Fanny Nisbet under a fig tree at Montpelier Plantation, then the couple sailed off to England and destiny.

Outside Charlestown the island's ring road passes a series of sandy coves. Four-mile-long Pinney's Beach has several restaurants catering to lunchtime swimmers and sunset drinkers; sheltered Oualie Beach looks out to St. Kitts across a two-mile channel; pristine Lover's Beach is edged by sea-grape trees. As the road curves to the windward coast it skirts the ruins of old estates, while offshore, Montserrat, Antigua and Guadeloupe shimmer on the horizon. At the south end of the island, the road climbs the flanks of Nevis Peak. Here rugged ravines, called 'ghauts', run to the sea, and green vervet monkeys, the descendants of pets brought by the French in the mid-1600s, haunt hiking paths. The Botanical Garden of Nevis has tamed a corner of this landscape, gathering exotic flora in a tropical setting. And everywhere coppers, boiling-houses and mills have been turned into inviting backdrops for convivial gatherings.

The best-known beach on easy-going Nevis, Pinney's (*opposite*) extends for four blissful miles – plenty of space to find one's own patch of palm-shaded sand and to dream of sailing the Caribbean's blue waters. French mariners more than 300 years ago brought green vervet monkeys here as pets. The animals have multiplied in the island's grasslands and rain forest, becoming pests to farmers but an attraction for visitors (*above*).

The copper kettles that once boiled cane juice show up as decorative objects in houses and gardens, like those at the Montpelier Plantation Inn (*right*), part of a historic eighteeenth-century manor and now a boutique hotel. Nearby, the Botanical Garden of Nevis (*below*) showcases seven manicured acres of palms, orchids, bromeliads and cacti from around the world.

Crumbling brick ruins and a towering chimney are all that's left
of a sugar factory at New River Estate (*above*), one of the many
plantations that flourished on Nevis, beginning in the 1600s.

At 3,232 feet high, Mount Nevis dominates the view from the teahouse at the Botanical Garden (*above*). The conservatory in the grounds is modelled on the building at Kew Gardens, but features screens instead of glass. Shutters frame a bluer view at the Nisbet Plantation Beach Club (*opposite*), which was built as a sugar plantation in 1778.

Wispy clouds breeze past the top of Mount Nevis (*opposite*), which looms over an old stone church. Columbus sighted a white veil over the peak and accordingly named the island with the Spanish word for snow. The wood-and-stone buildings that line Charlestown's Low Street (*above*) remind passers-by of Nevis's nineteenth-century heyday, when planters and merchants lived well on sugar wealth.

st kitts

On a late spring morning a field of ripe sugarcane is rippling in the breeze. Nearby, a cane train overflowing with the newly harvested crop heads down narrow-gauge tracks. The sugar industry may be waning on St. Kitts, but it still defines the view. Above the cane fields, the rain-forested slopes of Mount Liamuiga rise 3,792 feet. The volcanic origins of this extinct cone are reflected in the dark boulders of lava that have erupted at Black Rocks, on the wave-splashed drama of the windward coast.

Christopher Columbus sighted this 17-mile-long island – shaped something like a cricket bat – when he sailed past in 1493; he may also be responsible for its formal name, St. Christopher. But it wasn't until 1624 that the English established the first non-Spanish European colony in the Caribbean here. A year later a few French settlers joined them, and though the two groups tussled between themselves, they united to wipe out the indigenous Caribs in a massacre at Bloody Point.

The colonists started by planting tobacco and cotton, but by the mid-1600s sugar was king – produced on great estates worked by African slaves. St. Kitts prospered as a 'mother colony', with French and English planters moving on to other Leeward Islands. The connections spread beyond as well: at St. Thomas's Anglican church, the great-grandfather of U.S. President Thomas Jefferson is buried next to Thomas Warner, 'Governor of the Caribee'.

Over the next half-century the see-saw struggle for power in Europe was played out on St. Kitts, too, until the island had become wholly British by 1713. To protect its vast sugar wealth, the victors fortified Brimstone Hill with a series of magnificent bastions, barracks and retaining walls, turning it into a 'Gibraltar of the West Indies'. (It was named a World Heritage Site in 1999.) And though the French managed to dislodge the fortress's defenders after a siege in 1792, the Treaty of Versailles returned St. Kitts to the British, and it remained a colony till independence in 1983.

Today the capital city of Basseterre flanks the busy waterfront with a criss-cross of streets lined by two-storey buildings. The commercial centre is The Circus – a Caribbean version of London's Piccadilly around an ornate green clock monument. A block away, Independence Square was once a slave market; now it is bordered by the Catholic church, art galleries and nineteenth-century houses in various states of renovation. At the edge of town stands the St. Kitts Sugar Manufacturing Company, built in 1912. Each day during the three-month harvest, sugar trains shuttle the government-owned crop through steam-powered machinery, where it is crushed, milled, cured and crystallized, into syrup, molasses and sugar for shipment to England. The island's historic sugar mills and estates, however, have mostly been transformed into attractive inns, restaurants and art studios.

Sweeping lawns lead up to the generous verandas of the Great House at Ottley's Plantation Inn (*opposite*), part of an estate that dates back to 1690. The manor is now a country hotel, and its old stone dependencies have also been transformed into cottages. In the capital of Basseterre, a quirky clock-cum-monument stands at the centre of the Circus (*above*), the island's homage to London's Piccadilly. Many of the surrounding nineteenth-century buildings now house restaurants; the latticework balconies are ideal spots for keeping an eye on the comings and goings below.

The southern peninsula – which reaches toward Nevis, two miles away – also has new life. Once this hilly narrow strip was valued only for its salt-ponds. Today, the prize is its string of sandy beaches – Frigate Bay, Friar's Bay, and Banana and Cockleshell Bays – lively gathering spots all for twenty-first-century sun-worshippers who stay in the hotels and frequent the beach bars and restaurants, adding the next chapter to St. Kitts' own sweet story.

Dust flies as ripe sugarcane is cut (*opposite below left*) and tipped into carts for transport to Basseterre. One chimney still stands at the end of a canefield road (*opposite below right*). Pastel Creole-style houses enclose the Caribelle Batik workshop (*opposite above*) at Romney Manor, on the site of another historic plantation.

Sugar-fine sand is the attraction at the southern end of St. Kitts, where South Friar's Bay Beach (*left*) and Frigate Bay Beach (*below*) remain invitingly uncrowded – except for a collection of queen conch shells.

Overleaf A monument to eighteenth-century military engineering, Brimstone Hill Fortress has been called the Gibraltar of the West Indies. Massive walls topped by cannon enclose the Citadel, which has a commanding view inland to Mount Liamuiga as well as seaward to neighbouring islands. A museum inside explains the fort's strategic role during the struggle between Britain and France over their sugar-rich Caribbean possessions, as well as the decades-long renovation of this World Heritage Site.

st lucia

Picture twin peaks – neat verdant cones, one slightly slimmer than the other – rising above an azure sea. The Pitons are the unmistakable symbols of St. Lucia, depicted everywhere on the island, even lending their name to the local beer. Pushed up by magma beneath the earth's crust, they bear witness to the volcanic origin of the island. The geological story is most evident at Sulphur Springs, a huge collapsed crater in the south-west. Though it last exploded 140 years ago, steam still rises from vents in the earth, and mud prized for its therapeutic qualities bubbles nearby. The smell of sulphur permeates the air, accounting for the name – Soufrière – of the important historic town nearby.

The name is French, bestowed by settlers who arrived about 1650, after the Spanish, Dutch and the British failed to take St. Lucia permanently from the Caribs, who had lived there since A.D. 800. The British soon returned, however, and for 150 years the tear-shaped isle, 27 miles long and 14 wide, bounced back and forth fourteen times between the two European powers until it was firmly attached to the British Empire in 1814.

The French influence, however, lingers in the Creole style of cooking, the plaid madras cloth that brightens dress and décor, and the rapid-fire local patois. The English left a legacy of administration (since 1979 St. Lucia has been an independent member of the Commonwealth), driving on the left, cricket and the eighteenth-century ruins in Pigeon Island

National Park. Those fortifications near the island's northern tip overlook the popular beaches and sailing grounds of Rodney Bay, site of a great naval battle in 1782. Today, the battlements offer a superb panorama that reaches to Martinique.

The capital of Castries hugs its own deep harbour. On Saturdays its market is busy with farmers selling fruits and vegetables, and tourists browsing the arts-and-crafts stalls. On Sundays, the city's focus shifts to the Roman Catholic cathedral, where parishioners worship beneath the gaze of black religious figures pictured in the colourful murals by local artist Dunstan St. Omer. Outside, busts in a shady square honour St. Lucia's two Nobel Prize winners, economist Arthur Lewis and poet Derek Walcott.

In the centre of St. Lucia, lush rain forest cloaks the mountains, which are home to orchids and a rare parrot, attractions for bird-watchers and hikers. The volcanic soil produces tons of bananas, bountiful ground provisions like yam and dasheen, and an array of fruits and flowers, many of which are on display at the Diamond Botanical Garden and the historic working cocoa estate of Fond Doux. 'Take a leaf, drop it on a rock, and it will grow,' one kitchen gardener says, amazed. Along the coast, fishing sustains the villagers of Anse La Raye, Canaries and Dennery. More and more the turquoise sea attracts sailors, divers and snorkellers who explore the marine reserve at Anse Chastanet and the waters around Petit Piton.

St. Lucia's signature mountains, the Pitons (*opposite*) zigzag the horizon, memorable highlights of the mountainous terrain near the town of Soufrière. At 2,619 feet, the Petit Piton is actually about 150 feet taller than Gros Piton but has a slimmer silhouette. Hikers and rock climbers can tackle the volcanic cones' difficult slopes; divers and snorkellers can enjoy the marine life at their base. Almost any visitor to St. Lucia, however, can get close to the Pitons by hoisting a local beer (*above*).

Attached to the British Empire in 1814 and now an independent member of the Commonwealth, St. Lucia shows many signs of an English presence, typically in the islanders' enthusiasm for cricket (below). The French alternated with the British fourteen times for control of St. Lucia. One of their legacies is a profusion of Gallic placenames, including that of Anse La Raye (opposite), a simple fishing village, where a boat hull provides a youngster with a moment's entertainment.

st lucia **quiet gems**

THANKS BE TO GOD J6-653
DISCIPLE J6 235 ALR
REPENT AND BE BAPTIZED

Surprisingly delicate arches of wrought iron define the soaring space of the
Cathedral of the Immaculate Conception (*above*), where the murals painted
in 1985 by Dunstan St. Omer animate virtually every inch of wall. Constructed
in 1897, the Catholic church is in the centre of St. Lucia's capital, Castries,
which lost most of its colonial buildings to fires over the centuries. Soufrière
(*opposite*), which gets its name from still-active sulphur springs, dates back to
1746, and many more of its atmospheric wooden residences have survived.

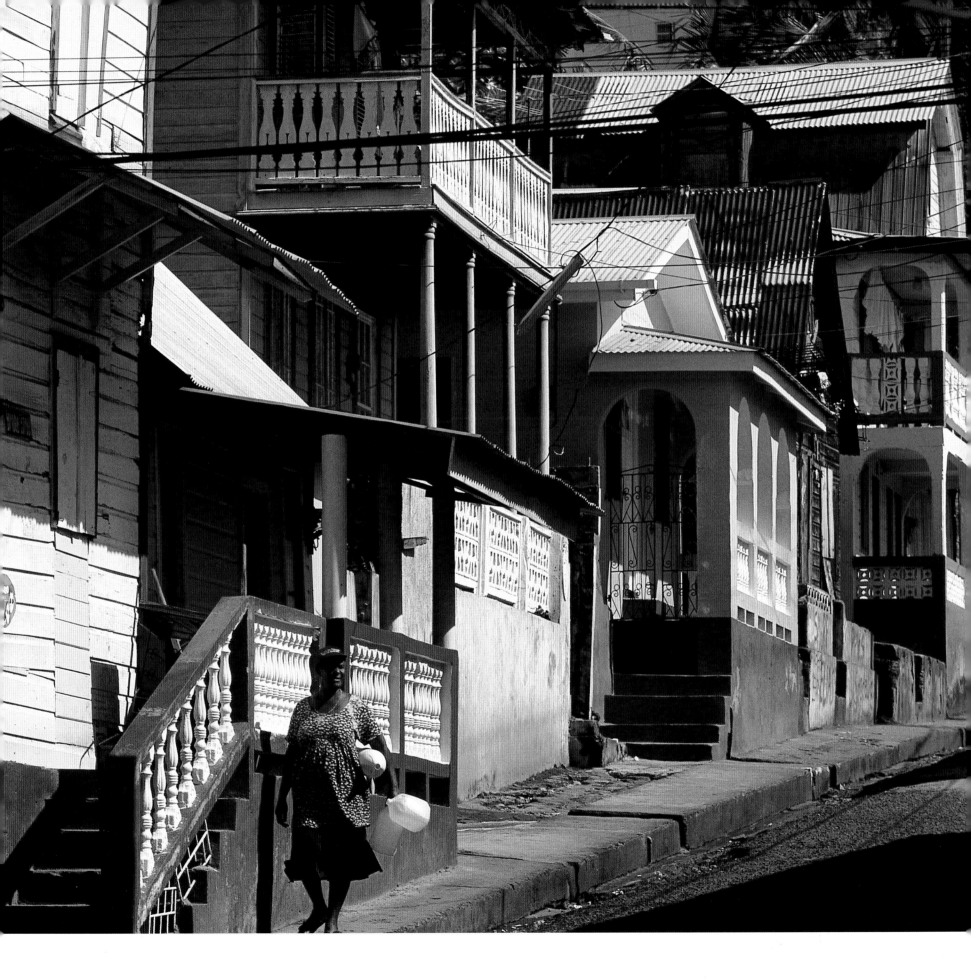

The Pitons dominate the view wherever you are in the south of St. Lucia: on a mountain road (*opposite*), gazing through the open 'fourth wall' of a room at Ladera Resort (*left*), or beachside between the peaks (*above*).

terre de haut

A statue of Marianne greets visitors who step off the new quay into the central square of Terre de Haut, and the French *tricolore* flies over the pastel *mairie*, the town hall, just up the street. Everywhere pastel, gingerbread-trimmed cottages abut chic boutiques and an occasional art gallery. This little island – a cluster of hills, bays and headlands roughly four miles long and three miles wide – is a stylish bit of France in the Caribbean. Together with its placid sister island of Terre de Bas, it makes up Les Saintes, part of the overseas *département* of Guadeloupe nine miles north.

Columbus sailed past here on All Saints' Day 1493, accounting for the islands' name. But today's inhabitants owe their heritage to colonists from the west coast of France, who claimed the isle in 1648. They brought a few slaves, but the place proved too dry for sugarcane, so plantations never really took hold here. Instead, the islanders – mostly light-skinned and blue-eyed – turned to fishing for their livelihood. Their catch now appears in the waterside restaurants along the beguiling main street of Le Bourg, Terre de Haut's town. The succulent seafood is served in countless forms: sliced thin and marinated, smoked for a salad, or seasoned with garlic and oil and grilled whole, often preceded by an appetizer of *accras de morue*, cod fritters.

Dominating the heights at one end of Le Bourg is the sturdy fortress of Fort Napoléon, named for the Emperor who commissioned it in 1809 but not finished until 1867. From its ramparts the panorama sweeps over the harbour, busy with ferries, fishing-boats and yachts. Today, the sparkling depths are favoured by divers, but in 1782 the roadway was the scene of the massive Battle of Les Saintes, in which British ships destroyed a French fleet. Even after that, control of these islands teetered back and forth, until the Treaty of Vienna in 1815 gave Les Saintes to France.

All this history is put into context at the fort's museum, along with exhibits on the early Carib inhabitants and displays of local boat-building, furniture and the creation of local crafts, such as the characteristic *salako*, the curious Asian-looking headgear fashioned from bamboo and covered with madras.

Meanwhile, there's a distinctive rhythm to life in Terre de Haut: ferries bring day-trippers in the morning and take them away again in late afternoon; in between, the visitors head for the beaches. Twice a day, fleets of scooters – few cars are allowed here – buzz through the streets as parents pick up their children for lunch and after school. And in the evening couples fill the bars and cafés, as they stop by to toast sunset with a rum-laced Planter's Punch.

Blue sea mirrors sky in the bay that fronts Le Bourg (*opposite*) on Terre de Haut, one of Guadeloupe's Les Saintes. The panorama is the reward for the walk up to Fort Napoléon, built for protection in the 1800s and now a museum. Outside its battlements a garden of cactus and succulents thrives in the dry climate; inside, dioramas depict the pivotal sea battle that took place here between French and British fleets in 1782. Today, instead of warships, fishing-boats ply the waters, supplying local restaurants, like the popular Le Genois (*above*).

Among the souvenirs prized by visitors is the *salako*, a type of hat supposedly brought from Asia generations ago. The bamboo-and-madras creations are made by craftsmen on the neighbouring isle of Terre de Bas (*below left*) and worn with aplomb on the streets of Le Bourg (*below right*).

The galleries, boutiques and restaurants of the waterfront town (*above*) are a favourite destination for day-trippers from 'the mainland', who swell the island's population of about 1,650. They share the streets with youngsters on their way to and from school (*opposite above*).

Sandy beaches and deep bays scallop the shore of Terre de Haut beneath its undeveloped hillsides (*left*). Beyond the clustered houses of Le Bourg a hiking trail leads to the highest rise, named Le Chameau (the Camel) for its humplike shape. Among the more unusual residences is a house built like a boat (*above*), the home and office of an island doctor.

the grenadines

Jewel-like stepping-stones in a turquoise sea, the thirty isles of the Grenadines extend south from the 'mainland' of St. Vincent, the administrative centre of the country, which earned independence from Britain in 1979. These waters are beloved by sailors, who have countless stunning anchorages – including Canovan, Mayreau, Union Island, Palm Island, Petit St. Vincent and especially the pristine wildlife reserve of the uninhabited Tobago Cays – to choose from.

Two islands epitomize the variety of the chain. Friendly Bequia, an hour's ferry ride from Kingstown, St. Vincent's capital, is the second largest island, but its roughly zigzag landmass is still just a compact seven square miles. Its original peaceful Arawak inhabitants succumbed to the warlike Caribs, who eventually were conquered by the French in the mid-1700s. The battlements that the Europeans fortified still overlook picturesque Admiralty Bay and the pastel shops and houses of Port Elizabeth. The British took over in 1783 and after a short era of dependence on sugarcane, the islanders turned to the sea – including whaling – for their livelihood. Bequian fishermen are still allowed to harpoon two whales a year, but the tradition mostly lives on in the model whaleboats carved by the island's master craftsmen, whose replica schooners also routinely fetch very high prices.

Roads and paths lead to inviting beaches – windward Industry Bay (where an islander has rescued and released hundreds of hawksbill

turtles over the last decade); Spring Bay, at the edge of an old coconut plantation; half-moon Friendship Bay; and Lower Bay Beach and Princess Margaret Beach, short water-taxi rides from town.

Visible from Bequia's southern side is Mustique, a plantation island acquired by Colin Tennant (Lord Glenconner) in 1958. He ran it as a private estate and in the 1960s added to its jet-set reputation by inviting a coterie of friends, including the late Princess Margaret, to build hideaway villas there. Celebrities such as Mick Jagger continue the tradition. The tiny isle – a mere mile by a mile and a half – is shaded by tamarind and flamboyant trees and blessed by spectacular beaches with sand like talcum powder and warm aquamarine waves. Macaroni Beach, Pasture Bay, Ansecoy Bay…take your pick!

The harbour at Britannia Bay welcomes day sailors and cruisers, who often stop to dine and drink at its famous watering hole, Basil's Bar and Restaurant.

And though Tennant no longer owns the island, it remains in private hands, with two small hotels and not quite a hundred villas. Many of these houses, whose architectural designs range from Balinese compounds and beachfront Palladian mansions to a clifftop Moroccan fantasy, are available for rent, providing a taste of the Caribbean as glittering as sun on sea.

The view from the porch of the aptly named Gingerbread Hotel (*opposite*) stretches beyond Bequia's Admiralty Bay to the hills where first the French and later the British manned a fort in the eighteenth century. These deep protected waters make the island a choice stopover among Grenadines yachties. The next landfall south is Mustique, where Basil Charles (*above*) welcomes celebrities and ordinary sailors alike to the bar that bears his name.

Waves of fun send a couple of young islanders back on to Bequia's Lower Bay Beach (*below*) as a water-taxi zips by. The rainbow-coloured vessels deliver visitors to swimming and snorkelling spots south of Port Elizabeth.

A private gazebo in the green hills (*left*) has a good vantage point out towards Admiralty Bay. A charter sailboat (*below*) heads for a more distant anchorage. The thirty islands of the Grenadines offer options that range from the wildlife reserve of the undeveloped Tobago Cays to smart private resorts.

the grenadines **quiet gems**

Endeavour Bay shimmers beyond the lily pond (*opposite*) in the grounds of Mustique's Cotton House Resort.

A breezy veranda wraps around the stone-walled Cotton House (*left*), which indeed stored drying cotton centuries ago; these days the building is the hotel's elegant lounge and dining-room.

Wooden flights of fancy trim the eaves of the shops (*above and opposite right and left*) in Britannia Bay on Mustique. The private island, where Britain's Princess Margaret once had a home, is dotted with architectural showplaces, from Balinese villas to castles out of *The Arabian Nights*. Britannia Bay is the island's only anchorage and the low-key commercial centre, with Basil's Bar and Restaurant, stores for groceries and supplies and a few boutiques.

tobago

Magnificent frigate-birds wheel and soar over the battlements of Fort King George, where a rank of cannons points out to sea. This is a peaceful spot. Huge samaan trees shade the old stone powder magazine, and the newly refurbished officers' quarters now house the Tobago Museum. Inside, exhibits focus on the Amerindian inhabitants who were here when Columbus sighted land in 1498, as well as the European settlers who traded control of Tobago – a fat cigar of an island some 8 by 25 miles – over the next 250 years. Among the more unusual colonists were the Courlanders, from Latvia, who sailed up in 1642. The Dutch supplanted them, followed by the French, and later the British, who ruled after 1802. For a brief time in the 1700s sugarcane made the island rich. It was to protect the plantations' mountainous watershed that the Tobago Forest Reserve was set up in 1776, one of the oldest reserves in the Western Hemisphere.

The sugar is long gone. But a wealth of bird life is one happy result of Tobago's centuries-old environmental initiative. Blue-crowned motmots and orange-winged parrots are just a few of the 225 avian species. The offshore islets of Little Tobago and St. Giles are home to flocks of seabirds – red-winged tropic birds, noddies, terns and red-footed and brown boobies, among many others.

Lush botanic gardens add a bit of green to the workaday capital of Scarborough. From there, roads fan out across south-western Tobago to tranquil bays, beaches and resorts that attract vacationers from nearby Trinidad – the two islands have been linked since 1888 and formed an independent country in 1976 – as well as from North America and Europe. One road leads to Buccoo Bay, an unassuming village by day but home to the boisterous Sunday School, a weekly late-night party. Buccoo also hosts the annual Goat Races, a rollicking Easter tradition in which the owners run along with the leashed contenders.

Other traditions persist on this friendly, relaxed island. Small kiosks near Pigeon Point serve Tobago specialities like curried crab and dumplings, and at the village of Castara local women bake bread and coconut-filled pastries in communal ovens twice a week. At Great Courland Bay, fishermen still haul in their catch with large seines pulled from the beach.

Pristine beaches scallop the shore. On the Atlantic side Bacolet Bay was once the haunt of Hollywood stars, who filmed several movies here in the late 1950s. On the calmer Caribbean coast are Mount Irvine Back Bay, accessible only on foot; Englishman's Bay, a narrow crescent of pale sand; and Parlatuvier Bay, dotted with fishing-boats. Heading north, a circular road hugs Tobago's shore, then crosses the forested spine. Hiking trails lead inland to sparkling waterfalls, and at the tip of the island Charlotteville edges Man o' War Bay. Not far away, Speyside, which overlooks Batteaux Bay, has become a centre for divers and snorkellers who want to explore its spectacular reefs. The marine Japanese Gardens teem with gorgonians, tube sponges, huge brain coral, sea fans and a profusion of colourful fish, mirroring the many winged species that enliven the skies above.

Fishing-boats bob off the beach at Castara Bay (*opposite*), one of countless sandy coves that dot the perimeter of Tobago, a frequent weekend haunt for residents of sister island Trinidad. A post-storm sunset at Stonehaven Bay (*above*) brings island dreams to life in glorious Technicolor.

Villagers in Great Courland Bay haul in the catch from shore with a traditional seine (*below*). Those who participate get some of the bounty.

Offshore fishing sustains the quiet village of Charlotteville (*left*), where houses cling to the steep hillside. In the late 1700s the British built Fort King George and its powder magazine (*above*) outside the capital of Scarborough; the city's Botanic Gardens (*top*) are a pleasant urban oasis.

A window into Tobago's hospitality frames a cook at Jemma's Sea View Restaurant (*opposite*), which serves home-style meals near Speyside. Also sure to raise a smile is a sassy painted wood sculpture (*below*) by artist Luise Kimme, who has filled her fanciful house-museum with memorable secular and religious figures carved from oak and cypress. Palm fronds and pots of flowers bring spots of colour to the white sands of Pigeon Point (*left*), where water sports and food stalls also enliven the scene.

adventurers' delights

bonaire

dominica

saba

st john

turks & caicos

virgin gorda

The excitement of harnessing wind and waves brings wind-surfing enthusiasts to the shallow waters off Sorobon Beach in Bonaire. Active travellers encounter many choices on the island – kite-surfing, kayaking, and, of course, diving in the world-famous National Marine Park.

bonaire

You see the divers everywhere – donning their gear by the side of the road, chatting on the piers near the dive centres or preparing to submerge near the buoy markers that denote each of the eighty-odd dive sites around Bonaire. Scuba enthusiasts from all over the world come to enjoy the pristine underwater environment – a colourful world of coral reefs and teeming marine life that has been zealously safeguarded by the Bonaire National Marine Park since its inception in 1979.

The boomerang-shaped island – 24 miles long and at most 7 miles wide– did not always seem so appealing. Its arid landscape is dotted with cactus and pitted with salinas. Of the first settlers, a group of Arawaks called Caiquetios, little is left except some stone artifacts and enigmatic rock paintings at Boca Onima. In 1499 the Spanish arrived; though they built a settlement inland at Rincon, away from marauding pirates, they thought the island 'useless' and never really took hold there. The Dutch came to stay, however, claiming Bonaire in 1633 and bringing African slaves to cut dyewood and harvest sea-salt, to preserve their precious herring. A handful of stark slave huts still stand as reminders of those harsh times.

These days Bonaire belongs to the Netherlands Antilles, a self-governing part of the Kingdom of the Netherlands. Islanders speak their own language, Papiamento, a mix of Dutch, Spanish, English, Portuguese, African and Amerindian tongues. And the centre has shifted to Kralendijk, a laid-back town with Dutch-style architecture, a deep-water cruise-ship dock and a bustling restaurant scene, especially at sunset.

Up and down the placid west coast bright yellow boulders mark famous dive sites with names like Andrea, Thousand Steps, Hilma Hooker and Angel City. Offshore, brilliant shadings of blue define the continuous fringing reef that slopes to about 30 feet, then drops dramatically to 130 feet. In the north, the coast road turns inland and passes briny Gotomeer, home to many of Bonaire's several thousand flamingos, the national bird; then it leads to the Washington-Slagbaai National Park. You can follow a ring road past forbidding limestone terraces, where dramatic waves crash and explode, to the lighthouse at Malmok and to Boka Slagbaai's old harbour, a nice spot for a picnic or snorkel. Small green parrots flit and dart around the slopes of Mount Brandaris, 784 feet high, which dominates the centre of the park.

The southern leg of Bonaire is defined by great salt-pans, condensing basins that produce gleaming mountains of salt for export. These, too, are favourite breeding grounds for flamingos, which sometimes rise at dusk in a great whoosh of wings to feed in nearby Venezuela.

The mangroves edging shallow Lac Bay serve as marine nurseries, which kayakers can explore. But out on the bay wind-surfers rule, manœuvring their neon-coloured sailboards like so many skittering insects. You can also watch them jump the waves from the beach at Cai. Here, in the shadow of towering mounds of conch shells – the remains of long-ago harvests – an energetic Creole band invites islanders and visitors alike to dance the Sunday afternoons away.

White peaks of salt (*opposite*) rise from salinas just south of Kralendijk, Bonaire's capital. The Dutch began developing the salt-pans here in the early 1600s to obtain a preservative for their precious herring. The island still exports more than 400,000 tons of the crystals. Along the north coast, waves fan out into Boka Cocolishi (*above*), a beachy cove in the Washington-Slagbaai National Park.

A modern mariner's landmark, the Kralendijk lighthouse (*left*), built in 1932, is part of Fort Oranje, which now houses Bonaire's court of justice.

In former times sailors watched for the orange obelisk (*right*), one of several markers on the southern coast. Just behind it are the squat huts that for weeks at a time sheltered slaves who worked the region's salt-ponds (*below*).

A mountain of conch shells, the remnants of long-ago harvests, catches the light at Cai (*above*). Gathering the mollusc is no longer permitted on Bonaire, where the emphasis is on maintaining a pristine, healthy environment. There's nothing wrong with toasting the sunset, though, a favourite pastime at Karel's Beach Bar (*opposite*).

Bonaire's ecotourism focus extends inland to the great Gotomeer lagoon (*opposite*), a feeding ground for its national bird. The long-legged flamingos have many congenial environments on the island, including the mangrove shallows near Lac Bay (*below*), in the south. More than 190 avian species live in the Washington-Slagbaai National Park, which features hiking trails up Mount Brandaris and diving and snorkelling at Boka Slagbaai (*right*).

dominica

Olive green, forest, moss and lime … sage, hunter, kelly, avocado … in Dominica the abundance of greens staggers the imagination. Though only a 16-by-29-mile oval, this 'nature island' is rumpled with majestic peaks – the highest Morne Diablotin at 4,747 feet – that hint at its recent volcanic origin. Much of its interior is protected in reserves, like Morne Trois Pitons National Park, declared a World Heritage Site in 1998. Here the lush rain forest vies with the geothermal wonders of Boiling Lake and the bubbling rainbow-coloured mud holes of the Valley of Desolation. There are rivers for every day of the year and a dozen major waterfalls. Trafalgar Falls boasts twin cascades, while the Emerald Pool is a delicate shower in a shadowed glade. Middleham Falls is the island's tallest, a breathtaking 200-foot drop.

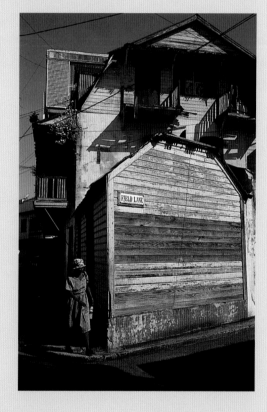

The island teems with exotic plants and animals: more than 170 kinds of birds, including four species of hummingbirds and two endangered parrots; 19 types of palms and 78 orchids; to say nothing of epiphytes, ferns and towering trees used for everything from house timbers to herbal cures. Tropical fruits of every kind are pressed to make the juices served in cafés and restaurants.

Because of Dominica's forbidding terrain, the indigenous Caribs were able to survive here after being eliminated from virtually every other Caribbean isle. A reserve established in 1903 along the island's east coast is home to about 3,000 of their descendants, who farm, fish and practice centuries-old crafts, like hand-carving canoes and weaving intricate baskets. The Caribs had been in Dominica, which they called Waitukubeli ('Tall is her body') for 100 years, when Columbus made landfall on Sunday, 3 November 1493. The Spanish didn't stay, however, and Dominica, after being passed back and forth between the French and the British, finally became a possession of the latter in 1805. The ruins of Fort Shirley, their eighteenth-century garrison, still overlook Prince Rupert Bay on the Cabrits headland in the north.

In 1978 Dominica gained independence and is now a member of the British Commonwealth. Its Gallic heritage (and the influence of neighbouring Martinique and Guadeloupe) lingers, however, in the islanders' French-influenced patois. The capital city of Roseau still displays remnants of the colonial era in its eighteenth- and nineteenth-century buildings with overhanging wooden balconies. The Old Post Office, next to Market Square, now houses the Dominica Museum, which recreates a Carib thatched hut and a merchant planter's living-room amid exhibits on natural history and the lime and cane plantations that once fuelled the economy. Out front a seaside promenade leads past the cruise-ship dock to the new market, where local farmers bring the bananas and ground provisions that dominate today's agriculture. Offshore, the pristine reefs are beginning to rival the rain forest as an attraction, as growing numbers of divers explore the marine reserve around Scott's Head.

Ribbons of water cascade into the Emerald Pool (*opposite*), at the end of a short forest hike. There are twelve major waterfalls on Dominica, as well as a dozen peaks more than 4,000 feet high and a network of hiking trails from easy to challenging, making the island an ecotourist's dream. A stroll around the capital, Roseau (*above*), takes visitors past rows of atmospheric wooden houses.

Morne Trois Pitons National Park (*left*) encompasses almost 17,000 acres of untouched green mountains, gorges and geothermal phenomena. The variety of landscapes on the island helps account for a wealth of animals, including four kinds of hummingbirds and two rare parrots. Undersea life thrives among the pinnacles and reefs of Scott's Head/Soufrière Marine Reserve, whose waters are visible in the distance from the Fort Young Hotel (*opposite*).

Local artistry finds an outlet on the wall of a bakery (*above*) that wants to advertise its wares in Roseau. More traditional crafts – carving a canoe from the trunk of a gommier tree (*opposite below left*) and weaving baskets with natural materials (*opposite above right*) – survive among inhabitants of the Carib reserve (*opposite above left*), whose features reveal their indigenous ancestry. The face of the future (*opposite below right*) looks sweet in island dress.

Built from volcanic stone, an eighteenth-century Roman Catholic church (*left*) stands on the beach in Soufrière, close to the vessels that characterize this small, south-west coast fishing village.

saba

An emerald mountain surrounded by sapphire waters, tiny Saba, just 5 miles square, is a pristine jewel treasured by divers and hikers. There's hardly any flat land; from the cloud-crowned peak of Mount Scenery, a dormant volcano 2,775 feet high, the slopes drop off sharply – no sandy beaches here – to deep-water seamounts just offshore. For generations the rugged landscape isolated islanders from the outside world and one end of the island from the other. All imported goods – from nails to pianos – had to be carried up hundreds of steep steps from Ladder Bay, the only place where boats could anchor. Finally, in 1943, a cement road was built, after a Saban named Josephus Lambert Hassell took an engineering correspondence course and supervised its construction by hand.

The divers discovered Saba's underwater riches in the late 1980s, and the establishment of the Saba Marine Park in 1987 has protected the patch reefs, sponge-encrusted walls, spires, ledges and volcanic pinnacles, along with its abundant sea life – from sharks and turtles to tiny seahorses. More recently a land-based national park was added, emphasizing the island's varied hiking paths. The stairway up Mount Scenery, notably, climbs through lush rain forest with elephant ears and tree ferns to an elfin cloud forest, where epiphytes drape the mahogany trees. Some trails cross grassy meadows and plunge through dry forests to offer bluff-top ocean views, while others follow the step-paths that once connected Saba's four charming villages.

The island's white-shingle cottages are trimmed with gingerbread, topped by red roofs, and hung with green shutters. A friendly attitude matches the quaint style. With just 1,600 residents, it seems that everyone knows everyone else; even short-time visitors soon recognize familiar faces. The village of Windwardside is Saba's social centre. It is also home to the Harry L. Johnson Museum, a 160-year-old sea-captain's cottage that pays homage to the traditional lifestyle of a century ago, when Saban men all went to sea and the women produced crafts to earn a little money. A framed christening gown shows off a fine example of the drawn-thread embroidery called Saba lace; a pump organ hints at home-grown entertainment.

The lowland village called The Bottom is the seat of government offices – the island was settled by the Dutch in the mid-1600s and has been officially part of the Netherlands since 1816 – and a medical school. Here, too, is the Church of the Sacred Heart, where local artist Heleen Cornet has decorated the nave, using Saban children as models for her angels and rain-forest flora for the plants of paradise.

Saba's flag – the golden star stands for the island, the blue for sea and sky – waves over The Bottom, the administrative centre of the island (*opposite*).

Divers from around the globe flock to Saba for its innovative Marine Park (*above*), established in 1987 and a showcase of spectacular coral and colourful fish.

Once only hiking paths connected the island's four villages, including The Bottom, nestled under Great Hill (*opposite*); in 1943 the islanders carved out a road by hand. For generations, until a jetty was built at Fort Bay, all goods transported here were carried up the long staircase at Ladder Bay.

In Windwardside much of the traditional architecture, such as Flossie's typical white cottage with green shutters (*below*), has been preserved. Local women get together in town to while away the hours making Saba lace (*both right*), actually drawn-thread embroidery. The intricate needlework, introduced in 1884 by an island woman who learned it at a convent school in Venezuela, was one way housewives could earn a little money while the men were away at sea.

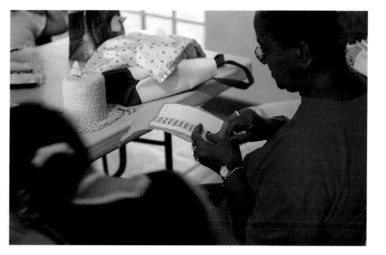

st john

The hiking trails of St. John – one of the U.S. Virgin Islands – are paths through history, revealing glimpses of the peoples who left their mark on its cactus-covered hills and spectacular blue bays. Petroglyphs carved between A.D. 1200 and 1400 are visible along the path to Reef Bay, the work of Taino Indians who lived here before Columbus sighted the island in 1483. Danish settlers arrived in 1718, drawn by a desire for profitable sugar plantations. The remains of their slaves' dwellings edge the old rocky roads, and the ruins of their sugar factories evoke the hard life and back-breaking labour of that era.

Sugar faded in importance after emancipation in 1848, and the United States acquired St. John, along with St. Thomas and St. Croix, in 1917. But it was millionaire Laurance Rockefeller who forged St. John's modern identity. He fell in love with the undeveloped island and bought two-thirds of its 21 square miles, then turned the land over to the U.S. Government to establish a national park that opened in 1956.

Today, ferries to neighbouring islands bustle in and out of little Cruz Bay at the western point of the arrowhead-shaped isle. Narrow twisting streets encompass popular restaurants and galleries decorated with latticework and gingerbread, while drivers slow their vehicles to lean out and chat with friends. Beyond the town, the North Shore Road climbs and drops, curves and climbs over the steep rises, past memorable white-sand beaches: Caneel Bay, where Laurance Rockefeller built a home (now part of a luxurious resort); the narrow strand of Hawksnest Bay; much photographed Trunk Bay, with its offshore snorkelling trail; and Cinnamon Bay, a gathering spot for water-sports fans. Beyond Maho Bay – where a tent camping complex epitomizes St. John's ecological approach – a road leads to the Annaberg Sugar Mill. Interpretative signs around the ruins explain the sugar-making process from the cane field to the boiling cauldron.

Eventually the road leads to Coral Bay, the island's original Danish settlement, and beyond, to the wilder East End peninsula, which faces the Sir Francis Drake Channel, a favourite sailors' passage. Here the British Virgin Islands extend to the horizon, so numerous that Columbus is said to have named them for St. Ursula's 11,000 companions. The way back to Cruz Bay follows the island's central ridge below the 1,277-foot peak of Bordeaux Mountain. All over the island scenic spots abound, happily for the growing number of bridal couples who find picturesque places to wed.

The crescent of Trunk Bay (*opposite*) is a well-known north-shore attraction, backed by the woodlands of the Virgin Islands National Park, which covers much of hilly St. John. Unbroken greenery has reclaimed the slopes where Danish settlers once grew sugarcane. Ruins of the Durloo Plantation sugar factory (*above*) add an eighteenth-century touch to Caneel Bay Resort, which is located on the old estate.

A forest of masts fills the lively harbour at Cruz Bay (*opposite*), but sailboats have to anchor further off the popular beach at Trunk Bay (*below*). A marked underwater trail there guides beginning snorkellers to the offshore islets. They can then explore on their own in Maho Bay (*right*), known for its green sea turtles, or off any of the other glistening beaches in the national park.

Schoolgirls pore over their homework on a snack-shop patio in Cruz Bay (*opposite*). The town is a social centre for locals and visitors alike, busy with shoppers during the day and thronged with diners and bar-hoppers at night. For solitude, hikers can follow the Reef Bay Trail (*below*) to a forest pool, where the rocks bear mysterious petroglyphs (*right*), then finish up the walk at a south-shore beach.

turks & caicos

The sea is a fantasy of blues flecked by the white foam of waves and bordered by the creamiest of sands. No wonder that the Turks and Caicos Islands have become a watery playground. Fishing and diving brought visitors here long before sun-worshippers discovered the spectacular beaches. The waters are rich with marine life: azure shallows harbour elusive bonefish; cobalt deeps are home to wahoo, tuna, marlin and shark. And the deeps are deep indeed. The 22-mile-wide Columbus Passage is a 7,000-foot dip in the seafloor, dividing the Turks Islands (Grand Turk and Salt Cay) from the Caicos (North, Middle, South, East and West Caicos and Providenciales).

Of the eight islands and forty cays, only ten are inhabited. Like the Bahamas, of which they are a geographical extension, they are mostly flat and arid. But there are differences among them. Middle Caicos has a long limestone ridge and a system of caves. North Caicos is far greener, with fruit trees and sugarcane fields and a lake that is home to dozens of flamingos. South Caicos is the base for a sport-fishing fleet and for divers who range over the Caicos Bank to harvest the queen conch, which appears on local menus in myriad ways, from chowder to ceviche, battered, cracked or jerked. Little Water Cay has become a nature preserve for some 3,000 iguanas. And tiny Salt Cay, with just sixty inhabitants, a few guest-houses and the glistening squares of old salinas, is known as 'the island that time forgot'.

It is salt that shaped the Turks and Caicos past. Lucayan Indians lived here centuries ago, but they were gone by the sixteenth century. Bermudans rediscovered the islands in the 1680s and brought their own African slaves to work the valuable salt-ponds. A century later British loyalists fleeing the American Revolution set up a few cotton plantations as well. All this history is recounted in the National Museum on Grand Turk, housed in one of the nineteenth-century residences that give the main street of this stringbean-shaped island such a quaint appearance.

Inside, along with Lucayan artifacts, there is a re-creation of a coral reef and exhibits about the ships that foundered on the dangerous shoals. One of those, the slave ship *Trouvadore*, was wrecked off East Caicos, but 192 freed Africans survived and joined the forebears of the 'belongers' who are today's islanders.

Grand Turk is also the administrative centre of the islands, which remain a British Crown Colony with a Governor appointed by the Queen. It is a tranquil place, with the comings and goings of dive boats providing the biggest splash. Most of the action has moved to once-quiet Providenciales – Provo for short – where condominiums and luxury hotels line the twelve talcum-sand miles of Grace Bay and sumptuous houses overlook the green islets of Chalk Sound National Park. In villages like Blue Hills, informal conch shacks still sit on the sparkling water's edge, but upscale hostelries are going up near wave-whipped North-West Point. And resorts also are rising on the outer islands. Elegant Parrot Cay, quiet Pine Cay and soon West Caicos and others will welcome visitors whose most strenuous activity may be the pursuit of pampering and the dreams of island living.

Since 1852 the Grand Turk lighthouse has stood on the worn cliffs of North-East Point (*opposite*). At first the beacon was lit with oil and tended by the keeper who resided in the one-room brick structure nearby; in 1894 the light was converted to kerosene. Now automated, it is still in use. On Providenciales – Provo for short – the foot-coddling softness of Grace Bay Beach (*above*) lightens any burden.

A deserted beach rims the north end of Grand Turk (*above*). Offshore the seafloor quickly drops to 7,000 feet in the Columbus Passage that separates the Turks from the Caicos Islands.

The varied depths of the region's seas account for the striking water colours. In Chalk Sound National Park, on Provo, light-blue shallows surround a dotted line of uninhabited cays (*right*).

Island fantasies start with unsullied sands and sparkling water, charms the Turks and Caicos Islands have in abundance – from fast-developing Grace Bay Beach (*opposite*) on Provo to the tranquil stretches of Grand Turk, where a dive boat anchors near Cockburn Town (*top left*) and a family takes an afternoon dip on Governor's Beach (*above left*). The celebrity retreat of Parrot Cay (*above right*) offers seclusion behind low sea-grass screens, but every sailor in Grace Bay (*top right*) can claim the ocean as his own.

A solemn ceremony for Remembrance Sunday – a commemoration of the soldiers of two world wars – brings out veterans and a police band (*all opposite*) to St. Mary's Anglican Pro-Cathedral (*above*) on Grand Turk. The church, built in 1900, fronts the main thoroughfare, which is lined with structures that reflect the island's heritage.

virgin gorda

On a quiet, sunny day the view of Virgin Gorda's North Sound reveals countless sailboats, one impressive yacht, one sunfish, one wind-surfer, one motor-launch, one kayak, another even more impressive yacht, more wind-surfers, and an entire islet devoted to a sailors' bar-restaurant. This British Virgin Island is indeed a waterman's haunt, and it has been since soon after Columbus sighted it in 1493.

Virgin Gorda sits at the eastern edge of Sir Francis Drake Channel, named for one of the buccaneers and pirates who navigated these brilliant blue waters in the sixteenth century. By the late 1600s the English had established cotton plantations here; after slavery ended in 1834, the settlers turned to other kinds of agriculture. More recently tourism – particularly sailing charters – has dominated the economy. More than a thousand sailboats are said to be available for rent in the British Virgin Islands, an Overseas Territory of some sixty isles and cays whose administrative centre, and largest landmass, is Tortola.

Virgin Gorda is the next biggest of the group. Roughly seven miles long, but squeezed to a narrow isthmus in several places, Virgin Gorda seems more like two distinct islands. In the centre 1,370-foot Gorda Peak towers over the landscape. From there, the road north rises steeply and dips around

Leverick Bay till it stops completely at Gun Creek. Beyond that point the resorts of North Sound are reachable only by boat. Offshore a host of other isles dot the horizon: private-resort Necker Island, the cruise-ship playground of Prickly Pear and the uninhabited Dogs, to name a few.

Southward from its hilly mid-section, Virgin Gorda flattens out with a series of inviting white-sand beaches – Mahoe Bay, Savannah Bay and Little Dix Bay – that attract bathers with their gentle waves. A crosshatch of sleepy streets makes up Spanish Town, where hundreds of masts fill the vast marina. The terrain turns dramatic again at craggy Copper Mine Point. There, ruins of a nineteenth-century copper works, once manned by Cornish miners, blaze red in the sun's rays.

Offshore, the uninhabited cay called Fallen Jerusalem sustains a wealth of many-hued reef fish. It is the exotic landscape of the south-west, though, that gives Virgin Gorda its distinctive look – and its fame. Huge granite boulders, like marbles flung by a race of giants, line the palm-fringed sands of The Baths. For sailboats this is a favourite anchorage, while swimmers and snorkellers delight in exploring the brilliant waters and their cathedral-like chambers.

Virgin Gorda's signature sight: the monumental granite boulders of The Baths at Devil's Bay National Park (*opposite*) are a famous sailor's destination; snorkellers can check out the cavern-like spaces among the rocks. A private walkway above the beach reveals many of the other British Virgin Islands lined up along the horizon. Water-lovers – of all ages and all kinds of vessels – flock to Virgin Gorda, including one young kayaker learning to paddle at the Bitter End Yacht Club (*above*).

Only light, lacy waves disturb the calm at Savannah Bay Beach (*opposite*), where the inviting aqua water harbours clusters of sea fans and soft corals. The *Spirit of Anegada* (*below*), a gaff-rigged schooner, offers seafaring thrills amid the islands and cays of the Sir Francis Drake Channel, named after the sixteenth-century buccaneer. Today, some estimate that 1,000 sailboats are available for charter in the British Virgin Islands.

Overleaf The secluded beach at Spring Bay adjacent to The Baths shares its tumbled-stone-and-palm seascape but not its throngs of visitors.

Page 162 Sea grapes ripen in the sun, adding a colourful touch to a boulder-edged shore. *Page 163* Other tropical details decorate a pastel façade at a North Sound resort.

something for everyone

cuba

dominican republic

jamaica

puerto rico

The pace of change moves slowly in Port Antonio, where Jamaica's tourists first came to the island aboard banana boats early in the twentieth century. The architecture on West Street retains the look of the Caribbean of those days.

165

cuba

Havana is the ageing seductress of Caribbean cities, her beauty fading, her apparel in tatters, but magnificent enough to inspire fervent passion. The capital of the largest island in the Caribbean and home to two million people, the city is a World Heritage Site, full of fabulous stone façades with columns and ornamentation, courtyards and balconies, some beautifully renovated, others on the brink of collapse. On the streets outside, American automobiles from the 1950s putter past, held together by scavenged parts and a keen spirit of improvisation. The old Buicks and Chevrolets in candy colours add to the sensation that time stopped in 1959, when the Cuban Revolution brought Fidel Castro to power.

A languid sensuality pervades the scene, a focus on the pleasures of the moment: eating, drinking and dancing to the music that is performed in hotels, bars, clubs, even street corners with foot-tapping artistry. Traditional *guajira*, *son* and *mambo*, *rumba* and *trova* – the irresistible rhythms have taken the world by storm. The roots of Cuban music reach back to the heritage of enslaved Africans. They arrived by the shipload, beginning in the early 1500s, to replace the indigenous Taino, who died off from disease and Spanish exploitation a few decades after Columbus first landed in 1492. As the colonists established settlements and searched for New World gold, Havana grew into a port for treasure convoys journeying back to Spain.

Many historic sights go back to those days. The Castillo del Morro, now a museum of Cuban history, was built in the late 1500s to guard the bay. The baroque limestone cathedral dominates an elegant square; even

older is the Plaza de Armas, lined by bookstalls and venerable edifices, including the Palace of the Captains-General, where the Spanish governors once lived. From the Plaza de Armas, a bustling pedestrian thoroughfare named Calle Obispo extends west towards monuments from the modern era – places associated with Ernest Hemingway, who is an icon on the island he loved.

Papa's drinking haunts are jammed with tourists. The cosy La Bodeguita del Medio is the place for a rum-and-mint *mojito*; at the fancier El Floridita a daiquiri is *de rigueur*. Like many famous visitors, Hemingway sometimes stayed at the Hotel Nacional, built in 1930 and still an evocative landmark, with galleries, gardens and a hotel pool that recalls the days when starlets lounged there half a century ago. Similarly unchanged is the Tropicana, an outdoor night-club where the skimpy costumes of the voluptuous dancers are counterbalanced by head-dresses that resemble glittering chandeliers.

Outside Havana much of the island remains quietly agricultural. Sugarcane, first planted in the early 1500s, has long shaped the destiny of the island, which had become the greatest sugar colony in the Caribbean by the early 1800s. The system – and the wealth – depended on slavery, which was only abolished in 1886, late in a century that saw weakening Spanish control, a growing push for autonomy and the first steps towards American involvement in Cuba's affairs. In 1895, an exiled lawyer, poet and journalist named José Martí headed an unsuccessful rebellion against the Spanish. Killed soon after fighting began, he is now revered as a national hero.

American automobiles from the 1950s, lovingly kept, add a frozen-in-time aura to the centuries-old streets of Old Havana (*opposite*), founded by the Spanish in the early 1500s. Citizens of a later age are memorialized in a sepia-toned mural (*above*). The historic part of the city is a UNESCO World Heritage Site, but it remains the vibrant centrepiece of the largest island in the Caribbean, and home to two million people.

Three years later an explosion on the battleship *Maine*, in Havana harbour, precipitated the Spanish-American War, and finally Cuba's independence in 1902.

The new country was ruled by strong men, notably Fulgencio Batista, whose increasingly corrupt and repressive dictatorship began in 1933 and lasted more than two decades. During those years vacationers flocked to the sensual island, drawn by spectacular beaches, glamorous hotels and gangster-run nightclubs and casinos. But poverty and inequality eventually fuelled the political unrest that culminated in the victory of Fidel Castro's guerillas on New Year's Day 1959. The Cuban Revolution brought the island into Cold War politics. After the United States supported the ill-fated Bay of Pigs invasion, Castro's increasingly close ties with Russia led to the Cuban Missile Crisis of 1962. For years afterwards, Russia poured huge subsidies into the island, until the collapse of the Soviet Union and a continuing American embargo left Cuba with shortages of food, fuel and consumer goods. Today, the world waits to see what the next chapter, politically and economically, will be.

Meanwhile, Cuba works its magic on thousands of visitors, even Americans, who are officially forbidden to 'trade with the enemy'. On an island more than 600 miles long and 75 miles wide, there is much to see beyond Havana. Beautiful beaches dot the coast; the best known is the white-sand peninsula of Varadero, a lively resort with dozens of international hotels. To the west of Havana are the verdant valleys and limestone hills of bucolic Viñales. This is tobacco country, where the aromatic leaves are grown and fashioned into the celebrated hand-rolled Cuban cigars. The city of Santiago de Cuba, in the far south-east, has its own wealth of museums and monuments and a vibrant musical tradition. Finally, there's the Isla de la Juventud, with a splendid beach, pristine dive sites, and the slow pace of horses and buggies that ply the streets of the island's main town, a fresh-faced country sister to Havana's sultry *femme fatale*.

Unmatched bell-towers flank the ornate, columned
façade of Havana's eighteenth-century cathedral (*above*),
where carts selling mementoes fill a lively plaza flanked by
upscale restaurants. The tile roofs and pastel façades of the
old city (*opposite left*) are an architectural treasure trove,
though many buildings need renovation. The domed capitol
(*opposite right*), visible from a window of the Hotel Sevilla in
central Havana, was erected in 1929, three decades before
Fidel Castro came to power. Today, the heroes of the Cuban
Revolution – dead and alive – are enshrined on the shelves
of an open-air bookstall in the Plaza de Armas (*right*).

The scantily clad girls of the Tropicana night-club (*above and left*) continue to strut their stuff, though many entertainments from the 1950s, like casino gambling, are long gone in Cuba.

Other islanders also make a living catering to tourists: in Old Havana women dressed in period costumes pose for photos (*above*) and a coachman conducts tours of the historic area (*above right*).

A young Cuban labours on a road crew (*right*) on the Isla de la Juventud, where a highway cuts a swath between stately palms (*page 173*). Striking limestone hills called *mogotes* (*overleaf*) dot pastoral Viñales, west of Havana, a valley known for its tobacco.

dominican republic

Kite-surfers wheel and jump, riding the wind and waves off the golden sands of Cabarete, on the Dominican Republic's Atlantic shore. The beach that first attracted French Canadian wind-surfers a decade or so ago is now a hip resort, overshadowing the fact that Columbus's flagship, the *Santa Maria*, was wrecked along this coast on Christmas Day 1492.

Isla Española– later Hispaniola– was the third island Columbus touched in his initial voyage, and his first settlements were here in the north, but in August 1496 the Spanish moved south to their new capital of Santo Domingo. Today that city's Colonial Zone, a World Heritage Site, is a collection of pastel architectural treasures and New World 'firsts'. In the centre is the Parque Colón, next to the limestone cathedral, the earliest in the New World. A few blocks away, at the edge of the five-hundred-year-old city walls, is the Fortaleza Ozama, constructed in 1505 by Governor Nicolás de Ovando, who brought order to the new colony but harshly killed off the indigenous Taino. The Calle Las Damas – the oldest street in the Americas – is named for the *señoras* who arrived in 1509. Fine residences line the thoroughfare: Casa de Bastidas, home of the colonial tax-collector; several townhouses – converted to an elegant hotel – owned by Ovando; the National Pantheon, originally an eighteenth-century Jesuit monastery; and the Museo de las Casas Reales, erected in the early 1500s for the governor and the royal court. At the end of the street stands the Alcazar de Colón,

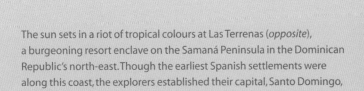

the gracious two-storey mansion of Columbus's son, Diego, restored with period furnishings.

Throughout the historic area vendors serve the fresh-fruit shakes called *batidas*, and kiosks dish up street snacks like *pastelitos*, filled turnovers, or *tostones*, fried plantain slices. The Colonial Zone is alive with islanders working, shopping, dining and drinking. It is an integral component of the sprawling urban metropolis that is home to some three million of the Dominican Republic's eight million inhabitants.

Like the population, the country is large, more than 18,000 square miles, two-thirds of the oblong island shared with Haiti. The politics of the two nations have been connected since the sixteenth century, when the French wrested control of the western region from the Spanish and founded a valuable sugar colony called Saint-Domingue. In the 1790s the Haitians rebelled against the French and in 1801 overran their Spanish neighbour, too. They dominated it again for two decades after 1822, a bitter time in the Dominican Republic, whose own independence came in 1844. The following century saw a succession of regimes and rulers. A brief period of re-annexation to Spain in 1861 was followed by the restoration of the republic in 1865, then by intervention by the United States in 1916 that lasted eight years. In 1930 Rafael Trujillo became president, and for thirty years ruled as a dictator until his assassination in 1961. Today the country is a democracy.

The sun sets in a riot of tropical colours at Las Terrenas (*opposite*), a burgeoning resort enclave on the Samaná Peninsula in the Dominican Republic's north-east. Though the earliest Spanish settlements were along this coast, the explorers established their capital, Santo Domingo, in the south; the city wall near the San Diego gate still stands (*above*). Nearby, the restored Alcázar de Colón, the sixteenth-century palace of Columbus's son, Diego, houses colonial Spanish furniture inside its arched façade.

Over the last two decades the Dominican Republic has turned to tourism, although simple villages still dot the interior, and fertile plains and valleys produce a variety of crops. In the east there is a dwindling sugar industry; in the central Cibao valley, banana plantations thrive, as do fields of rice and tobacco, whose leaves end up in prized hand-rolled cigars. The Cordillera Central dominates the middle of the island with imposing mountains, including the Caribbean's highest, Pico Duarte, at 10,417 feet. The climb to the top is a rigorous but rewarding two-day trek. Less energetic travellers head to the burgeoning resort areas. On the northern Amber Coast – named for the abundant fossil resin that is fashioned into jewelry – huge all-inclusive hotels overlook the water. The main town of Puerto Plata has a sixteenth-century fort and a pretty plaza with renovated nineteenth-century houses. Towards the east, inns and restaurants enliven Sosua, which welcomed German and Austrian refugees at the onset of World War II; beyond lies the water-sports mecca of Cabarete. Along the Caribbean coast, the highway east of Santo Domingo runs through small beach communities to exclusive Casa de Campo, where luxurious villas cluster around two world-class golf-courses, polo fields and a marina. At the sunrise tip of the island are the glistening beaches of Bavaro and Punta Cana, another expansive resort.

From October to January visitors can share the national passion for baseball; Dominican stars fill the roster of many major league teams in the United States. And all year long there is the seductive rhythm of *merengue*, which blares from music systems everywhere. Accompanied by accordion, *güira* (a cylindrical scraper) and *tambora* (a small drum), dancers turn the traditional two-step into a marvel of swirling skirts and suggestive hip movements with an exuberant vitality that erupts at a moment's notice.

dominican republic **something for everyone**

Ladies of the Spanish Viceroy's court would take their evening promenade along Calle Las Damas (*above*), the oldest paved street in the New World, in the heart of Santo Domingo's Colonial Zone. The thoroughfare is lined by townhouses from the 1500s, mostly museums and hotels today. At the end of the street stands Las Atarazanas, the historic shipyards that have been turned into shops and restaurants, including the Museo de Jamón (*opposite above*), where tasty ageing hams hang from the ceiling. Under traditional arches, decor takes on twenty-first-century flair in the lobby bar (*opposite below*) of the Casa Colonial hotel, in Puerta Plata.

Fresh fruit provides a ready snack all over the island: in the capital, a street
vendor (*above*) stays open day and night. And at a colourful kiosk in
Las Terrenas, everything from pineapples to papayas can be turned into
a frothy drink called a *batida* (*opposite*).

The graceful sixteenth-century Capilla de Nuestra Señora de Los Remedios (*opposite*) enclosed a family's private chapel; across the street, the imposing Museo de Casas Reales was the seat of the royal court. Since the 1500s islanders have worshipped in Santo Domingo's cathedral (*above*), the first to be built in the New World; its decorative gates (*left*) were added in 1992 for the 500th anniversary of Columbus's arrival here.

jamaica

'One love, one heart…': the infectious beat of *reggae* pulses through Jamaica like musical life-blood. For many people around the globe, *reggae* is Jamaica, and has been ever since Bob Marley burst upon the world music scene in the 1970s. His songs are virtual island anthems, as robust as Blue Mountain coffee, as smooth and powerful as Jamaican rum.

The third-largest island in the Caribbean, Jamaica is almost 150 miles from west to east and 51 miles across, with a population of 2.6 million people. Its fertile terrain ('Spit a seed and it will grow', locals say) rises to green hills that stretch almost the length of the island, culminating in the Grand Ridge of the Blue Mountains, topped by 7,402-foot Blue Mountain Peak. From the heights, broad rivers flow down to the sea: the Rio Grande emerges near Port Antonio; the Black River makes its way through swampland into Black River Bay; and the Martha Brae River lazes its way to Falmouth. There are scenic cascades, too, including stair-stepped Dunn's River Falls, and inviting YS Falls.

Edging the island are the beaches that attract most travellers today: the Oracabessa cove made famous in the film *Dr. No* – now known as James Bond Beach; Montego Bay's showpiece, Doctor's Cave Beach; the seven-mile stretch that brings spring-break revellers to Negril; and the black-and-white strands near Treasure Beach. One of Jamaica's wildest landscapes is called Cockpit Country, a region

of pitted limestone hills that once harboured escaped slaves known as Maroons, whose name, some say, comes from the Spanish *cimarrones*, or 'runaways'. The Spanish were the first Europeans in Jamaica; Columbus arrived at Discovery Bay, near Ocho Rios, in 1494, when the island was home to some 600,000 Tainos, who soon died out. The first settlement was on the north coast, but the capital later moved south, to what became Spanish Town. When the British conquered the island in 1655 – the Spaniards' departure is commemorated in place-names like Runaway Bay – they took over the city and put up refined Georgian-style buildings, including the first Anglican cathedral in the New World, around a central square.

During their campaign against the Spanish, the British enlisted the help of buccaneers, including Henry Morgan, who attacked ships and pillaged cities across the Caribbean. He ruled his pirates from the bawdy houses and grog shops of Port Royal, but later became Lieutenant Governor of Jamaica and died in his bed before the earthquake of 1692 caused the fabled 'wickedest city in the world' to sink beneath the sea. By the 1700s the British were battling the elusive Maroons, who lived in impenetrable mountain settlements, where they slow-cooked their spiced meats over pimento wood. The method lives on in 'jerked' pork, one of the mainstays of Jamaican cuisine, which includes the national dish of *ackee* (a tropical

A thatched-roof gazebo at the Half Moon Resort (*opposite*) offers a quiet spot for contemplating the seascape of Jamaica's popular north coast. Island visitors frequently toast the end of day with rum drinks (*above*), like these sun-kissed cocktails served at *Goldeneye*, the Oracabessa estate once owned by novelist Ian Fleming, the creator of James Bond.

Carefree spirits rule at Calabash Bay (*overleaf*), on the low-key south coast. The area's few hotels welcome travellers looking for a less-developed Jamaica, the kind of place where fishing-boats still pull up on the sands of a quiet cove (*page 185*).

fruit) with saltfish; spicy filled turnovers called *patties*; *bammies*, flat toasted cassava wafers; and *festival*, a fried doughnut-like bread. The favourite beverage, of course, is rum, a by-product of the sugarcane grown on the numerous plantations worked by African slaves. Once hugely prosperous, the estates foundered after emancipation in 1838, but a handful of historic manor houses, such as Rose Hall and Greenwood Great House, still evoke an eighteenth-century lifestyle.

In the late 1800s Kingston became the capital of Jamaica. Though few tourists visit the city, it remains a centre of artistic and intellectual life, home to the National Gallery, the Bob Marley Museum, theatres, shops, jazz-clubs and restaurants. After independence from Britain in 1962, Jamaican culture captured the world's attention, first with *ska* music, then with *reggae*, which drew strength from the Rastafarian religion that promoted a 'back-to-Africa' philosophy and, in the process, popularized dreadlocks and the use of marijuana. Tourists had discovered Jamaica

long before, though. Early in the twentieth century celebrity visitors started to arrive in Port Antonio aboard banana boats; that resort's reputation was enhanced by the presence of Errol Flynn, who supposedly came up with the idea of using bamboo river rafts for pleasure excursions. Novelist Ian Fleming had a house, *Goldeneye*, near Oracabessa. One of his guests, playwright Noel Coward, liked the area so much he built his own home, *Firefly*, on a hillside with an unparalleled view past the coast's serrated cliffs to the Blue Mountains.

In the last few decades, resorts have blanketed the north shore, from the cruise port of Ocho Rios to the large hotels and superlative golf-courses of the Montego Bay area, all the way to Negril. That town, once a bohemian hangout, is now a mix of all-inclusives, small guest-houses and boutique properties. On its long white sands, beach bars come to life after dark with bands that create an open-air party, and clubs rock till morning with tourists and locals alike.

Located in the midst of a private plantation, the impressive tiers of YS Falls (*opposite*) end in a tropical swimming hole framed by ginger. Jamaica's varied terrain is rich in rivers, which cascade from the island's mountainous centre to the sea. Reach Falls (*left below*) emerges from a lush green gorge south of Port Antonio (*left centre*), where a kayaker takes an aqueous route past the area's gracious homes. More modest architecture prevails in a village near Black River (*left above*), the waterway that flows through the south coast swampland called the Great Morass.

Long supple branches arc above a country road near Middle Quarters known as Bamboo Avenue (*opposite*) for its trademark trees. Their shape is echoed in the gingerbread-trimmed gables of a house in Buff Bay (*above*). At Harmony Hall (*right*), near Ocho Rios, the art extends inward from the architectural tracery; the old Methodist manse from the mid-1800s is now a gallery for the works of Caribbean painters and sculptors.

puerto rico

From the battlements of the El Morro fortress the view takes in a blue bay and a modern city skyline. But the massively thick walls and huge bulwarks instantly recall the might of sixteenth-century Spain, for which this fort was a crucial guardian of sea-lanes plied by convoys laden with New World wealth. Between this bastion and the San Cristóbal fort lies today's walled quarter of Old San Juan, a grid of stone-paved streets around a serene cathedral.

Two bustling squares, Plaza de Armas and Plaza de Colón, are flanked by delicious pink, lime and powder-blue houses with arched windows, wrought-iron balconies and interior courtyards. Among them is a treasure trove of colonial architecture: notably, the Dominican monastery from 1523; the Fortaleza, the governor's mansion built in 1540; the sixteenth-century Casa Blanca, home to the Ponce de León family; the seventeenth-century Alcaldía, or city hall; and the Capilla del Cristo, an eighteenth-century chapel.

In 1493, when Columbus first claimed the island, it was home to bands of Taino Indians, who were ruled by chiefs and who worshipped spirits called *zemis*. Some of their ritual sites have survived, including one at Caguana, where rock-slab petroglyphs surround fields for ceremonial ball games. The island they inhabited – the smallest and easternmost of the Greater Antilles – is 110 miles long by 35 miles wide, with a volcanic cordillera across the middle from east to west. In the north, limestone karst country is penetrated by an extensive series of caves. All around the island, the highlands slope to a coastal plain generously rimmed by sandy beaches. And in the north-east at El Yunque National Park, plentiful waterfalls add grace notes to the towering rain-forest flora.

Ponce de León established the first European settlement in 1508. Thirteen years later he moved his capital to what is now Old San Juan, where he ruled as Governor. Over the next century the colony was fortified and withstood attacks by English buccaneers like Francis Drake and, later, Dutch invaders. But Spain maintained its control and gradually brought in African slaves to work the fields. The Catholic Church, too, grew more influential, as friars spread the religion to outlying villages. At San Germán, Dominicans founded a monastery and in 1606–7 built a chapel – the oldest religious sanctuary outside San Juan – that now houses a museum of religious art.

A distinct Puerto Rican culture also sprang up, combining Amerindian, Spanish and African heritages. It is evident today in a calendar-crowding profusion of local festivals commemorating saint's days and crafts like mask- or lace-making, reflected in the unique *plena* and *bomba* music and *danza* compositions. Island cuisine tickles the palate with garlicky stews and gumbos, endlessly varied plantain and yam dishes, and *comida criolla*, featuring shrimp and pork. To drink, of course, there is always high-quality rum. The latter is a product of the sugar industry that dominated

Peach, pink and buttercup hues add a delectable flavour to the Old World architecture along narrow Calle Las Monjas (*opposite*), one of the atmospheric streets that lead down from the cathedral in historic San Juan.

The nineteenth-century buildings in Ponce, Puerto Rico's second city (*above*), have a rival to their pastel colour scheme in nature's palette.

agriculture in the 1800s, particularly in the south, near Ponce. Puerto Rico's second city was founded in 1692, but it really burgeoned in the nineteenth century. A wealth of superb buildings – the cathedral, the ornate Teatro La Perla and the unforgettable red-and-black-striped firehouse – cluster in its historic district around the Plaza las Delicias.

The Spanish-American War of 1898 ended colonial rule here and the island was ceded to the United States, to which it still belongs today, but with its own Governor and legislature. It is a modern island of almost four million people – American citizens since 1917 – laced by freeways, dotted by malls and shopping centres and supported by a range of pharmaceutical, high-tech and other industries, including tourism. Large luxury hotels, particularly on the north coast, cater to visitors seeking busy casinos and notable golf-courses. There is good diving in the west, south and east and off the isles of Vieques and Culebra. Rincón, in the west, attracts surfers who enjoy the waves and the easy-going beach atmosphere.

San Juan itself, long a cruise-ship port, has blossomed into a sophisticated destination with fine museums, shopping, old-style coffee bars, glamorous restaurants and music and dance clubs that pulsate into the small hours with an entrancing island beat.

Established in 1510, Puerto Rico's capital was laid out with its main square at Plaza de Armas (*right*). The Alcaldía, the city hall built between 1604 and 1789, is just one of the elegant buildings that flank the popular gathering spot for families and their feathered friends. Pigeons find a cosy cote in Parque de las Palomas (*opposite*), which sits atop the city wall that defines Old San Juan.

A mighty fortress, El Morro (*above*) was built in 1591 on a strategic point of land between the Atlantic and San Juan Bay. Wrought iron and stained glass add ornamental details to the nineteenth-century Casa de los Kindy (*opposite*), in San Germán, home to an array of well-preserved churches and residences from the last five centuries.

After dark the crowds disperse from the Plaza de Armas (*left*), leaving the fountain statues, representing the four seasons, alone at centre stage. The hip San Juan crowd heads for drinks at Nono's (*above*), in a colonial-style building overlooking Plaza San José.

An explosion of waves delights bathers at a tidal pool at Playa Caracoles (*above*) on the north coast, near Aricibo. The force of water is evident all over Puerto Rico: in the rain forest of El Yunque (*opposite right*), La Coca Falls breaks through the dense greenery. At the Parque de las Cavernas del Rio Camuy, an underground river has carved out an extensive cave network; waterfall sprays there bathe the moss-lined walls (*opposite bottom left*). Not far away, at Caguana, indigenous Taino Indians built a ceremonial centre, laying out a series of ritual ball courts edged by stone slabs with enigmatic petroglyphs (*opposite top left*).

travellers' guide

While every effort has been made to ensure that the information given in the following entries is correct, the author and the publisher cannot be held responsible for any inadvertent inaccuracies. The Travellers' Guide is not intended to be a conventional guide, but is based on the author's tastes and preferences. Conventional guidebooks should be consulted if further information is required.

Antigua 15

For more information: Antigua and Barbuda Department of Tourism, corner of Nevis Street & Friendly Alley, P.O. Box 363, St. John's, Antigua W.I., + 1 268 462 0480, www.antigua-barbuda.org

HOTELS

Blue Waters Hotel, + 1 268 462 0290, www.bluewaters.net. Comfortably upscale beach-front all-inclusive resort on Boon Point.

Carlisle Bay Antigua, + 1 268 484 0000, www.carlisle-bay.com. New, urban-style luxury resort on the south coast.

Coco's Antigua, + 1 268 460 2626. Elegant West Indian-style bungalows on a water-view bluff near Jolly Harbour.

Copper and Lumber Store Hotel, + 1 268 460 1058, www.copperlumberantiguahotel.com. Twelve-room hotel in a restored eighteenth-century building within Nelson's Dockyard.

Curtain Bluff Resort, + 1 268 462 8400, www.curtainbluff.com. Long-established all-inclusive luxe resort, emphasizing tennis and water sports, on the south coast.

Galley Bay, + 1 268 462 0302, www.eliteislandresorts.com. High-end all-inclusive resort in a garden setting on the beach in Five Islands.

Long Bay Hotel, + 1 268 463 2005, www.longbayhotel.com. Island-style cottages on Long Bay.

RESTAURANTS

Catherine's Café, + 1 268 460 5050. Simple but stylish French food on a deck overlooking English Harbour.

Abracadabra, + 1 268 460 1732. Lively trattoria in English Harbour.

Big Banana-Pizzas in Paradise, + 1 268 480 6985. Good pizzas and salads in restored Redcliffe Quay in St. John's.

Long Bay Hotel Beach Bar, + 1 268 463 2005. Open-air lunch place on the sand at Long Bay.

Seabreeze Café, Falmouth Harbour Marina. Sandwiches and gelati on the dock in Falmouth Harbour.

Bahamas Out Islands 63

For more information: The Bahamas Ministry of Tourism, P.O. Box N-3701, Nassau, Bahamas, + 1 242 302 2000, www.bahamas.com

HOTELS (HARBOUR ISLAND)

Bahama House Inn, + 1 242 333 2201, www.bahamahouseinn.com. Seven-room bed-and-breakfast in an eighteenth-century house in Dunmore Town.

Coral Sands, + 1 242 333 2350, www.coralsands.com. Bluff-top, ocean-view accommodation on Pink Sand Beach.

Dunmore Beach Hotel, + 1 242 333 2200, www.dunmorebeach.com. Fourteen water-view cottages on Pink Sand Beach.

Pink Sands, + 1 242 333 2030, www.pinksandresort.com. Luxe resort with 25 cottages and fanciful Balinese décor, on Pink Sands Beach.

Rock House, + 1 242 333 2053, www.rockhousebahamas.com. Boutique hotel in Dunmore Town.

Sugar Apple Bed and Breakfast, + 1 242 333 2750, www.redapplebb.com. Comfortable self-catering accommodation a few minutes' walk from the beach.

The Landing, + 1 242 333 2707, www.harbourislandlanding.com. Seven atmospheric rooms in two early nineteenth-century houses.

HOTELS (ELEUTHERA)

Unique Village, + 1 242 332 1830, Pleasant beach-front accommodations in Palmetto Point.

HOTELS (ELBOW CAY/GREEN TURTLE CAY)

Bluff House Beach Hotel, + 1 242 365 4247, www.bluffhouse.com. Romantic hilltop water-view rooms and villas on Green Turtle Cay's White Sound.

Green Turtle Club and Marina, + 1 242 365 4272, www.greenturtleclub.com. Water-oriented resort on White Sound.

Hopetown Harbour Lodge, + 1 242 366 0095, www.hopetownlodge.com. Colourful rooms and cottages in historic Hopetown on Elbow Cay.

RESTAURANTS (HARBOUR ISLAND)

Arthur's Bakery and Café, + 1 242 333 2285. Coffee and fresh pastries in Dunmore Town.

Hammerhead's Bar and Grill. Light meals overlooking the Marina.

Sip Sip, + 1 242 333 3316. Lunch in a casual chic cottage overlooking Pink Sand Beach.

Harbour Lounge, + 1 242 333 2031. Seafood and island dishes on the Dunmore Town waterfront.

Rock House, + 1 242 333 2053. Lunch in the garden and gourmet dinners in an elegant dining-room.

The Landing, + 1 242 333 2707. Fine Euro-Bahamian cuisine in a historic house.

RESTAURANTS (ELEUTHERA)

Pina Café. Sandwiches and snacks in Governor's Harbour.

RESTAURANTS (GREEN TURTLE CAY)

Macintosh Restaurant and Bakery, + 1 242 365 4625. Local dishes in a casual restaurant in New Plymouth.

Jolly Roger, + 1 242 365 4247.
Waterfront bar-bistro at the Bluff House Beach Hotel.

Barbados 23

For more information: Barbados Tourism Authority,
Harbour Road, Bridgetown, Barbados, + 1 246 427
2623, www.barbados.org

HOTELS

Almond Beach Club and Spa, + 1 246 432 2115,
www.almondresorts.com.
Beach-front, service-oriented all-inclusive resort,
on the west coast, near Holetown.

Casuarina Beach Club, + 1 246 428 3600,
www.casuarina.com.
Apartment hotel in a lush garden setting, on the
south coast's Dover Beach.

Cobblers Cove, + 1 246 422 2291,
www.barbados.org/hotels/cobblers.htm.
Luxurious suites on a west-coast cove
near Speightstown.

Sandy Lane Hotel & Golf Club,
+ 1 246 444 2222, www.sandylane.com.
Palladian-style ultra-luxe hotel with a spa and
45 holes of golf, on the west coast.

Villa Nova, + 1 246 433 1524,
www.villanovabarbados.com.
Former house of Sir Anthony Eden, now an intimate
country house hotel, near the east coast.

RESTAURANTS

Atlantis Hotel, + 1 246 433 9445.
Bajan specialities at Sunday lunch, in Bathsheba.

Carambola, + 1 246 432 0832.
Romantic west-coast cliff-side setting for Caribbean-
French cuisine.

Cliff House, + 1 246 432 1922.
Spectacular multilevel water-side
restaurant with an innovative menu,
in St. James.

Daphne's, + 1 246 432 2731.
Sophisticated beach-side restaurant serving
contemporary Italian dishes on the west coast.

Josefs, + 1 246 420 7638.
International cuisine in a restored Barbadian house
on the south coast.

Waterfront Café, + 1 246 427 0093.
Seafood and Caribbean dishes, and occasional jazz,
in a lively bistro in Bridgetown.

Bonaire 123

For more information: Tourism Corporation Bonaire,
Kaya Grandi #2, Kralendijk, Bonaire, Netherlands
Antilles, + 599 717 8322, www.infobonaire.com

HOTELS

Bellafonte, + 599 717 3333,
www.BellafonteBonaire.com.
Ocean-front three-storey Mediterranean villa with
one- and two-bedroom suites.

Buddy Dive Resort, + 599 717 5080,
www.buddydive.com.
One-, two- and three-bedroom apartments in a
full-service dive resort.

Captain Don's Habitat, + 599 717 8290,
www.habitatbonaire.com.
Cottages, apartments and suites in Bonaire's
pioneering dive resort; dive packages are emphasized.

Friar's Inn, + 599 717 3948, www.friarsinn.com.
A colourfully decorated backpackers' bed-and-
breakfast, in the centre of Kralendijk.

Harbour Village Beach Resort, + 599 717 7500,
www.HarbourVillage.com.
Luxurious rooms and suites on a white-sand beach,
next to Bonaire's marina.

RESTAURANTS

Angel Floating Restaurant, + 599 717 4514.
Local specialities on a one-of-a-kind boat-restaurant,
moored at the Kralendijk city dock.

Casablanca, + 599 717 4433.
Lively Argentinian grill.

City Café, + 599 717 8286.
Popular breakfast, lunch and late-night spot on the
Kralendijk harbour.

Karel's Beach Bar, + 599 717 7434.
Sunset drinks and music at weekends.

Mona Lisa, + 599 717 8718.
Cosy Dutch-style bar and restaurant.

Richard's, + 599 717 5263.
Seafood specialities in a waterfront setting.

Rose Inn, + 599 785 6475.
Creole and island cooking in a garden setting
in Rincon.

Zeezicht, + 599 717 8434.
Long-time island favourite emphasizing seafood,
across from the harbour in the heart of Kralendijk.

Cuba 167

For more information: Cuba Tourist Board,
1200 Bay Street, Suite 305, Toronto, Ontario, M5R 2A5
Canada, + 1 416 362 0700, www.gocuba.ca

HOTELS

Hotel Florida, + 53 762 4127.
A nineteenth-century merchant's mansion in Old
Havana, converted into a 21-room business hotel.

Hotel Inglaterra, + 53 733 8593.
A landmark hotel in Central Havana with intricate
tilework in the lobby.

Hotel Nacional de Cuba, + 53 733 3564,
www.hotelnacionaldecuba.com.
A famous atmospheric throwback to the Havana
of the past.

Hotel Santa Isabel, + 53 733 8201.
A seventeenth-century building overlooking
Havana's Plaza de Armas, with 27 rooms furnished
with Spanish colonial furniture.

Hotel Sevilla, + 53 760 8560.
A grand Moorish-style hotel near the Parque Central.

Parque Central, + 53 766 6627,
www.nh-hoteles.es.
Modern, comfortable and convenient hotel located
on the central Havana park that gives it its name.

RESTAURANTS

Adela, + 53 732 3776.
Paladar (tiny private restaurant) set in an artist's house.

El Aljibe, + 53 724 1584.
Criollo fare in Havana's upscale Miramar area.

El Floridita, + 53 733 8856.
Well-appointed bar-restaurant in central Havana,
associated with Hemingway, known for its daiquiris.

El Patio, + 53 761 8504.
Criollo cuisine in a lovely colonial house on the Plaza
de la Catedral in Old Havana.

La Bodeguita del Medio, + 53 762 4498.
A bustling bar-restaurant in Old Havana and favourite
place to toast Ernest Hemingway with a mojito.

Curaçao 31

For more information: Curaçao Tourist Board,
19 Pietermaai, P. O. Box 3266, Willemstad,
Curaçao, Netherlands Antilles, + 599 9 434 8200,
www.curacao-tourism.com

HOTELS

Avila Beach Hotel, + 599 9 461 4377,
www.avilahotel.com.
Long-established family-owned hostelry, centred
on a historic Dutch colonial mansion, once the
Governor's residence.

Curaçao Marriott Beach Resort and Emerald Casino,
+ 599 9 736 8800, www.Marriotthotels.com/curmc.
Beach-side resort ten minutes from
downtown Willemstad.

Floris Suites, + 599 9 462 6111,
www.florissuitehotel.com.
Euro-style ten minutes from downtown Willemstad.

Howard Johnson Plaza Hotel, + 599 9 462 7800,
www.curacaohowardjohnson.com.
Conveniently located on the Otrobanda
side of St. Anna Bay.

Kura Hulanda, + 599 9 434 7700,
www.kurahulanda.com.
Luxurious village-style boutique hotel composed
of renovated historic dwellings and shops in
Otrobanda, with a museum and conference centre.

RESTAURANTS

Blues Beach Bar & Restaurant,
+ 599 9 461 4377.
Locals' hangout with Thursday night jazz and
blues at the Avila Beach Hotel.

Fort Nassau, + 599 9 461 3450.
Overlooking Willemstad, a good place for a sunset
drink with a view.

Gouverneur de Rouville, + 599 9 462 5999.
Lunch, dinner and an evening pub on the
Otrobanda waterfront.

Havana Cafe, Brionplein.
Coffee and pastries in a historic building on the
waterfront in Otrobanda.

Jaanchie's Restaurant, + 599 9 864 0126.
Island cuisine in an open-air setting with aviaries
at Westpunt.

Jaipur, + 599 9 434 7700.
Elegant Indian and Thai cuisine in a garden.

Plasa Bieu, in the Old Market in Willemstad.
Hearty local specialities cooked over wood fires;
lunch only.

Villa Elisabeth, + 599 9 465 6417.
Elegant haute cuisine, served in a nineteenth-
century villa and garden.

Dominica   131

For more information: National Development
Corporation, P.O. Box 293, Roseau, Commonwealth
of Dominica, + 1 767 448 2045, www.dominica.dm

HOTELS

Calibishie Lodges, + 1 767 445 8537,
www.calibishie-lodges.com.
Six Creole cottages around a pool and restaurant
on a hillside on the north coast.

Exotica, + 1 767 448 8839,
www.exotica-cottages.com.
Wood-and-stone cottage resort with organic gardens
and orchards in the hills outside Roseau.

Fort Young Hotel, + 1 767 448 5000,
www.fortyounghotel.com.
Upscale resort built around a historic military battery
at the edge of the Roseau waterfront.

Garraways Hotel, + 1 767 449 8800,
www.garrawayhotel.com.
Business hotel on the bayfront in Roseau.

Habitation Chabert, + 1 767 445 7218,
www.habitationchabert.com.
Intimate, art-filled luxury hotel with a river-side
garden on the east coast near Marigot.

Sutton Place Hotel, + 1 767 449 8700,
www.avirtualdominica.com/sutton.
Eight-room hotel with a basement jazz club,
in the heart of Roseau.

RESTAURANTS

Ancient Capital, + 1 767 440 2789.
Chinese dishes one block from the seaside walkway
in Roseau.

Indian River Cuisine, Portsmouth.
Creole specialities, not far from the Indian River.

La Robe Creole, + 1 767 448 2896.
Upscale dining in a renovated cottage in Roseau.

Miranda's Corner, Mount Joy, Springfield.
Roadside café with great juices and snacks.

Pearl's Cuisine, + 1 767 448 8707.
Island cuisine in the second-floor dining-room
of a historic house in Roseau.

Dominican Republic   175

For more information: Dominican Republic Ministry
of Tourism, www.dominicanrepublic.com/Tourism

HOTELS

Casa Colonial, + 1 809 320 2111, www.vhhr.com.
Fifty-suite luxury hotel on the beach at
Puerto Plata.

Hotel Francés, + 1 809 685 9331,
www.accor-hotels.com.
Nineteen luxurious rooms around a courtyard
in a converted sixteenth-century building in
Santo Domingo's Colonial Zone.

Hotel Palacio, + 1 809 682 4730,
www.hotel-palacio.com.
Former property of a nineteenth-century president
of the Dominican Republic, with 40 upscale rooms
in the Colonial Zone.

Piergiorgio Palace Hotel, + 1 809 571 2626,
www.piergiorgiohotel.cm.
Victorian-style hotel overlooking Sosua Bay.

Sofitel Nicolas de Ovando, + 1 809 686 6590,
www.sofitel.com.
Elegant hotel in an exquisitely renovated building
from 1502 in Santo Domingo.

RESTAURANTS

Bobos, + 1 809 689 1183.
Contemporary bar in the Colonial Zone in
Santo Domingo.

Café Conde de Penalde, + 1 809 688 7121.
Open-air café opposite the Parque Colón in
Santo Domingo.

Museo de Jamón, + 1 809 688 9644.
Ham and tapas specialities on the square in front
of the Alcazar in Santo Domingo.

Mesón Bari, + 1 809 687 4091.
Café and bar and old-time literary hangout in the
Colonial Zone.

Morua Mai, + 1 809 571 3303.
Seafood and pasta in the centre of Sosua.

Grenada   71

For more information: Grenada Board of Tourism,
Burns Point, P.O. Box 293, St. George's, Grenada,
West Indies, + 1 473 440 2279,
www.grenadagrenadines.com

HOTELS

Bel Air Plantation, + 1 473 444 6305,
www.belairplantation.com.
Luxurious Caribbean-style cottages overlooking
a marina at St. David's Point.

Laluna, + 1 473 439 0001, www.laluna.com.
Hip Balinese décor on a secluded beach at
Morne Rouge.

La Sagesse, + 1 473 444 6458,
www.lasagesse.com.
Quiet beach-side rooms around an old-style manor
house in St. David's.

True Blue Bay Resort, + 1 473 443 8783,
www.truebluebay.com.
Comfortable cottages in a lively marina setting,
across from St. George's University.

Grand Vue, Beausejour (Carriacou), + 1 473 443 6348.
Small hotel with a view of Hillsborough and
the harbour.

RESTAURANTS

Aquarium, + 1 473 444 1410.
Seafood specialities on a secluded beach.

Beach House, + 1 473 444 4455.
Seafood in an open-air restaurant on the beach
along the airport road.

Belmont Estate, + 1 473 442 9524.
Grenadian specialities in an open-air restaurant
on a working nutmeg and cocoa plantation
in St. Patrick.

Coconut Beach, + 1 473 444 4644.
French Creole dishes on the sand at
Grand Anse.

Deyna's Tasty Foods, + 1 473 440 6795.
Island cooking near the market in St. Georges.

Tropicana, + 1 473 440 1586.
A locals' favourite at the edge of St. Georges.

Tout Bagay, + 1 473 440 1500.
West Indian specialities, overlooking the harbour
in St. Georges.

Callaloo (Carriacou), + 1 473 443 8004.
Seafood and island cuisine, on the beach
in Hillsborough.

Turtle Dove (Tyrell's Bay, Carriacou).
Pizza and pasta.

The Grenadines 107

For more information: St. Vincent & the Grenadines
Ministry of Tourism and Culture, Cruise Ship
Terminal, Harbour Quay, Kingstown, St. Vincent &
the Grenadines, + 1 784 457 1502,
www.svgtourism.com

HOTELS (BEQUIA)

Creole Garden Hotel, + 1 784 4588 3154,
www.creolegardens.com.
Comfortable hillside studios overlooking Lower
Bay, with a West Indian restaurant called Dawn's
Creole Garden.

Frangipani Hotel, + 1 784 458 3255,
www.frangipanibequia.com.
A family home restored as an inn, plus garden-view
rooms, on the harbour at Admiralty Bay.

Gingerbread Hotel, + 1 784 458 8380,
www.gingerbreadhotel.com.
Romantic rooms looking out on Admiralty Bay.

Old Fort, + 1 784 458 3440,
www.theoldfort.com.
Several rooms in a converted eighteenth-century
fortified estate house in Mount Pleasant.

Spring on Bequia, + 1 784 458 3414,
www.springonbequia.com.
Hillside rooms overlooking an old coconut
plantation on Spring Bay.

HOTELS (MUSTIQUE)

Cotton House, + 1 784 456 4777,
www.cottonhouse.net.
Twenty luxe rooms centred on a converted
cotton drying house.

Firefly, + 1 784 488 8414, www.fireflymustique.com.
Intimate 4-room guest-house.

Mustique Villa Rentals, + 1 784 488 8000,
www.Mustique-island.com.
Fabulous villas on a private island.

RESTAURANTS (BEQUIA)

Coco's Place, + 1 784 458 3463.
Bar and restaurant with a great view of Lower Bay.

De Reef.
Beach-side lunches on Lower Bay Beach.

Fernando's Hideaway, + 1 784 458 3758.
Island dishes in Lower Bay.

L'Auberge des Grenadines, + 1 784 458 3201.
Lobster specialities on the Admiralty Bay waterfront.

Le Petit Jardin, + 1 784 458 3318.
Fine French food in a garden in Port Elizabeth.

RESTAURANTS (MUSTIQUE)

Basil's Bar, + 1 784 488 8350.
Famous harbour-side watering hole.

Jamaica 183

For more information: Jamaica Tourist Board,
64 Knutsford Boulevard, Kingston 5, Jamaica, West
Indies, + 1 876 929 9200, www.visitjamaica.com

HOTELS

Country Country, + 1 876 957 273,
www.countrynegril.com.
Fourteen brightly painted neo-Creole cottages
with beach access in Negril.

Courtleigh Hotel, + 1 876 929 9000,
www.courtleigh.com.
Comfortable six-storey hotel in Kingston.

Goldeneye, + 1 876 975 3354,
www.islandoutpost.com.
A luxurious private compound comprising Ian
Fleming's house and several chic one-, two- and three-
bedroom villas overlooking a quiet cove in Oracabessa.

Jamaica Inn, + 1 876 974 2514,
www.jamaicainn.com.
An elegant West Indies-style boutique hotel on a
pretty beach in Ocho Rios.

Rockhouse, + 1 876 957 4373,
www.rockhousehotel.com.
Sixteen faux-rustic cottages on the cliffs overlooking
the sea in Negril.

Round Hill, + 1 876 956 7050,
www.roundhilljamaica.com.
Upscale water-side rooms with plantation décor plus
hillside villas near Montego Bay.

Tensing Pen, + 1 876 957 0387,
www.tensingpen.com.
Thatched-roof stone cottages on a water-side cliff
in Negril.

The Caves, + 1 876 957 0269,
www.islandoutpost.com.
Ten individually decorated luxury wood-and-thatch
cottages on a cliff overlooking the Caribbean in Negril.

Wyndham Rose Hall Resort and Country Club,
+ 1 876 953 2650, www.wyndham.com.
Large Montego Bay beach resort with a water park
and extensive sports facilities.

RESTAURANTS

Hungry Lion, + 1 876 957 4486.
Nouveau Jamaican food in an art-filled cottage
in Negril.

Moonraker Bar and Grill, + 1 876 975 3663.
Open-air bar on James Bond Beach.

Norma's, Negril, + 1 876 957 4041; and Norma's On the Terrace, Kingston, + 1 876 968 5488. Creative local and regional dishes from a notable Jamaican chef.

Scotchie's, + 1 876 953 3301.
Jerk specialities in the Montego Bay area.

Sweet Spice, + 1 876 957 4621.
Island home cooking in an informal Negril setting.

Martinique 39

For more information: Comité Martiniquais du Tourisme, Immeuble Le Beaupré – Pointe de Jaham, 97233 Schoelcher, Martinique, + 596 596 61 61 77, www.martinique.org

HOTELS

Cap Est Lagoon Resort and Spa,
+ 596 596 54 88 01, www.capest.com.
Asian-Caribbean-style suites in a luxe hotel with gourmet cuisine on a beach near Le François.

Habitation Lagrange, + 596 596 53 60 60, www.habitation-lagrange.com.
Antique-filled rooms in a restored manor house.

Sofitel Bakoua Coralia, + 596 596 66 02 02, www.sofitel.com.
Luxury 133-room resort hotel across the bay from Fort-de-France.

RESTAURANTS

Café LaVague, + 596 596 78 19 54.
Casual water-side restaurant in St. Pierre.

La Grange Inn, + 596 596 66 01 66.
Casual bar-restaurant with a veranda in the Creole Village at Pointe du Bout.

Le Bambou + 596 596 52 39 94.
Country-style restaurant serving fish and Creole cuisine, on the rain-forest road at Fond Marie-Reine.

Le Ponton du Bakoua, + 596 596 66 05 45.
Open-air deck, serving sophisticated fish and island dishes in Pointe du Bout.

Le Touloulou, + 596 596 76 73 27.
Beach-side restaurant with island cuisine in Sainte-Anne.

Nevis 79

For more information: Nevis Tourism Authority, Main St., Charlestown, Nevis, + 1 869 469 7550, www.nevisisland.com.

HOTELS

Four Seasons Resort Nevis,
+ 1 869 4691111, www.fourseasons.com.
A luxe resort on Pinney's Beach, bordered by an 18-hole golf-course.

Golden Rock Plantation Inn, + 1 869 49 3346, www.golden-rock.com.
Sixteen rooms centred on an 1801 sugar plantation, surrounded by a nature reserve.

Montpelier Plantation Inn & Beach Club,
+ 1 869 469 3462, www.montpeliernevis.com.
A sophisticated 17-room plantation resort.

Mount Nevis Hotel & Beach Club, + 1 869 469 9373, www.mountnevishotel.com.
Small, contemporary resort on a hillside.

Nisbet Plantation Beach Club, + 1 869 469 9325, www.nisbetplantation.com.
Thirty-eight-room, restored manor house resort on the beach.

Oualie Beach Hotel, + 1 869 469 9735, www.oualie.com.
Easy-going cottages on sheltered Oualie Beach.

The Hermitage, + 1 869 469 3477, www.hermitagenevis.com.
West Indian-style guest cottages plus a 300-year-old Great House.

RESTAURANTS

Botanical Garden of Nevis, + 1 869 469 3399.
Martha's Teahouse serves lunch and dinner.

Café des Arts, + 1 869 469 7098.
Garden setting, connected to an art gallery.

Eddy's Restaurant & Bar, + 1 869 469 5958.
Local hangout upstairs in downtown Charlestown.

Sunshine's Beach Bar, + 1 869 662 8383.
Grilled lobster and fish on Pinney's Beach, famous for Painkiller cocktails.

Puerto Rico 191

For more information: The Puerto Rico Tourism Company, La Princesa Building, #2 Paseo La Princesa, Old San Juan, Puerto Rico 00902, + 1 787 721 2400, www.gotopuertorico.com

HOTELS

Casa Isleña, + 1 787 823 1525, www.casa-islena.com.
Nine-room beach-front inn in Rincón.

El Convento, + 1 787 723 9020, www.elconvento.com.
Luxury hotel in a restored Dominican convent in Old San Juan.

Hotel Milano, + 1 787 729 9050, www.hotelmilanopr.com.
Comfortable hotel in the centre of Old San Juan.

The Gallery Inn, + 1 787 722 1808, www.thegalleryinn.com.
Art-filled rooms in a converted hacienda in Old San Juan.

The Horned Dorset Primavera, + 1 787 823 4030, www.horneddorset.com.
Exquisite rooms and villas on the beach on the west coast in Rincón.

The Water Club, + 1 787 728 3666, www.waterclubsanjuan.com.
Sophisticated boutique hotel with superb views across from Isla Verde beach in San Juan.

Wyndham El San Juan Hotel & Casino,
+ 1 787 791 1000, www.wyndham.com.
Long-time luxury resort hotel in San Juan's Isla Verde area.

RESTAURANTS

Aguaviva Seaside Latino Cuisine, + 1 787 722 0665.
Trendy seafood in Old San Juan.

Baru, + 1 787 977 5442.
Puerto Rican specialities in a lively café in Old San Juan.

El Bombonera, + 1 787 722 0658.
A venerable café in Old San Juan.

King's Cream Ice Cream, Plaza de Delicias.
A long-standing ice-cream shop in Ponce.

La Fonda del Jibarito, + 1 787 725 8375.
Casual, family-run restaurant in Old San Juan.

Mi Casita, + 1 787 791 1777.
Puerto Rican dishes in a comfortable café in the Isla Verde section of San Juan.

The Horned Dorset Primavera, + 1 787 823 4030.
Prix-fixe four-course gourmet meals in Rincón.

Tamboo Seaside Grill, + 1 787 823 8550.
Burgers and salads overlooking Sandy Beach in Rincón.

Saba 139

For more information: Saba Tourist Office, P.O. Box 527, Windwardside, Saba Dutch Caribbean, + 599 416 2231, www.sabatourism.com

HOTELS

Ecolodge Rendez-Vous, + 599 416 348,
www.ecolodge-saba.com.
Twelve environmentally friendly cottages at
the edge of the rain forest near Windwardside.

El Momo Cottages, + 599 416 2265,
www.elmomo.com.
Seven simple cottages, a 10-minute walk
from Windwardside.

Juliana's Hotel, + 599 416 2269,
www.julianas-hotel.com.
A small, comfortable hotel with ocean views,
in the heart of Windwardside.

Queen's Gardens, + 599 416 3494,
www.queensaba.com.
Twelve luxurious suites, plus a pool and romantic
dining-room, with a superb view of The Bottom.

Scout's Place, + 599 416 2740,
www.sabadivers.com.
A long-established 30-room hotel with a dive
centre and friendly bar.

Willard's, + 599 416 2498,
www.willardsofsaba.com.
Seven well-appointed rooms with a spectacular
Caribbean view, as well as a tennis-court and a pool,
2,000 feet up, near Windwardside.

RESTAURANTS

Brigadoon, + 599 416 2380.
Varied menu in a house setting; a Windwardside
favourite.

Gate House Café, + 599 416 2416.
French and Creole dishes in a relaxed café in Hell's
Gate; an extensive wine list.

Rainforest Restaurant, + 599 416 3348.
Elegant meals in an ecolodge restaurant,
using produce from its own organic garden.

Saba Treasures.
Pizza and sandwiches in a stone-walled pub on
the main street in Windwardside.

YIIK, + 599 416 2539.
Second-storey, open-air café serving lunch and
dinner in Windwardside.

St. Barthélemy   47

For more information: Office Municipal du Tourisme,
Quai Général de Gaulle, Gustavia 97133
Saint-Barthélemy, + 590 590 27 87 27,
www.st-barths.com or www.frenchcaribbean.com

HOTELS

Eden Rock, + 590 590 29 7999,
www.st-barths.com/eden-rock.
Luxurious hotel on a bluff above Baie de Saint-Jean.

Hotel Guanahani, + 590 590 27 6660,
www.leguanahani.com.
Elegant Caribbean-style cottage resort on the beach
in Grand Cul-de-Sac.

Hotel La Banane, + 590 590 52 0300,
www.labanane.com.
Sophisticated boutique hotel at Baie de Lorient.

Hotel St. Barth Isle de France, + 590 590 27 6181,
www.isle-de-france.com.
Luxury boutique hotel on the beach at Baie
des Flamands.

Le Toiny, + 590 590 27 8888,
www.letoiny.com.
Ultra-luxe, secluded villas above Anse à Toiny.

SiBarth Real Estate, + 590 590 29 8890,
www.sibarth.com.
A wide variety of private villas for rent.

Village Saint-Jean Hotel, + 590 590 27 6139,
www.villagestjeanhotel.com.
Stone-and-wood cottages in a small, family-owned
hotel above Baie de Saint-Jean.

RESTAURANTS

La Gloriette, + 590 590 27 7566.
Fresh fish and Creole dishes in a relaxed beach-side
café in Grand Cul-de-Sac.

La Mandala, + 590 590 27 9696.
Thai-influenced French cuisine on a terrace with
a superb view over Gustavia.

Le Do Brasil, + 0590 590 29 0666.
Easy-going Brazilian-inspired restaurant on Shell Beach.

Le Select, + 590 590 27 8687.
Bar and garden watering hole made famous by the
Jimmy Buffett song, 'Cheeseburger in Paradise'.

L'Esprit de Salines, + 590 590 52 4610.
Varied menu in a chic, relaxed garden setting, on the
way to Anse de Saline.

Nikki Beach, + 590 590 27 6464.
Hip bar-restaurant on Baie de Saint-Jean.

Route des Boucaniers, + 590 590 27 7300.
Seafood on the water in Gustavia.

The Hideaway, + 590 590 27 6362.
Pizza and casual meals in Saint-Jean.

St. John   143

For more information: U.S. Virgin Islands Department
of Tourism, www.usvitourism.vi

HOTELS

Battery Hill, + 1 340 693 8692,
www.batteryhill.com.
Eight 2-bedroom condominiums overlooking
Cruz Bay.

Caneel Bay, + 1 340 776 6111,
www.rosewood-hotels.com.
Luxury rooms on expansive grounds,
once the property of Laurance Rockefeller,
with seven beaches.

Gallows Point Resort, + 1 340 776 6434,
www.GallowsPointResort.com.
Luxurious Caribbean-style suites on the edge
of Cruz Bay.

Maho Bay Camps, + 1 340 776 6240, www.maho.org.
Ecologically oriented tent cottages within Virgin
Islands National Park.

Westin Resort and Villas, + 1 340 693 8000,
www.westinresortstjohn.com.
Full-service resort on Great Cruz Bay.

RESTAURANTS

Asolare, + 1 340 779 4747.
Euro-Asian dishes, with a sunset-view terrace,
on the north-shore road.

Banana Deck, + 1 340 693 5055.
Seafood specialities upstairs, at the edge
of Cruz Bay.

Compass Rose Restaurant and Bar,
+ 1 340 777 3147.
Open-air cafe with a sunset panorama.

Donkey Diner, Coral Bay.
Congenial café, especially for Sunday breakfast.

Lime Inn, + 1 340 779 4199.
Fish dishes, a lively locals' favourite in Cruz Bay.

Paradiso, + 1 340 693 8899.
American cuisine in stylish Mongoose Junction.

St. Kitts   87

For more information: St. Kitts Tourism Authority,
Pelican Mall, Bay Road, P. O. Box 132, Basseterre,
St. Kitts, W.I, + 1 869 465 4040,
www.stkitts-tourism.com

HOTELS

The Golden Lemon Inn and Villas,
+ 1 869 465 7260, www.goldenlemon.com.
Colourfully decorated rooms in a Great House
or villas on Dieppe Bay.

Ocean Terrace Inn, + 1 869 465 2754,
www.oceanterraceinn.net.
Comfortable 78-room hotel, centrally located
at the edge of Basseterre.

Ottley's Plantation Inn, + 1 869 465 7234,
www.ottleys.com.
Plantation-style hotel overlooking the sea.

Rawlins Plantation Hotel & Restaurant,
+ 1 869 465 6221, www.rawlinsplantation.com.
Ten cottages in restored sugar plantation buildings.

St. Kitts Marriott Resort, + 1 869 466 1200,
www.stkittsmarriott.com.
Megaresort and condo complex on Frigate Bay.

RESTAURANTS

Fisherman's Wharf, + 1 869 465 2754.
Fresh seafood on the water.

Monkey Bar.
Lively open-air restaurant on Frigate Beach.

Sprat Net, + 1 869 465 6314.
Fish and local specialities, particularly at weekends,
north of Basseterre.

StoneWalls, + 1 869 465 5248.
Dinner in a hip indoor garden in downtown Basseterre.

St. Lucia 93

For more information: St. Lucia Tourist Board,
P. O. Box 221, Sureline Building, Vide Bouteille,
Castries, St. Lucia, + 1 758 452 4094, www.stlucia.org.

HOTELS

Anse Chastanet Resort, + 1 758 459 7000,
www.ansechastanet.com.
Luxurious, individualized rooms with views of the
Pitons, at the edge of a marine reserve near Soufrière.

Auberge Seraphine, + 1 758 453 2073,
www.aubergeseraphine.com.
Small hotel overlooking Vigie Yacht Marina in Castries.

BodyHoliday LeSport, + 1 758 457 7800,
www.thebodyholiday.com.
All-inclusive resort in a garden setting, emphasizing
sports, health, fitness, and extensive spa facilities at
Cap Estate.

Jalousie Resort and Spa,
+ 1 7588 456 8000,
Deluxe Caribbean-style cottages on the beach
between the Pitons.

Ladera Resort, + 1 758 459 7323,
www.ladera-stlucia.com.
Luxe hillside one- and two bedroom suites,
with an open wall and spectacular Pitons views
above Soufrière.

Sandals Regency St. Lucia Golf Resort & Spa at La Toc,
+ 1 758 452 3081, www.sandals.com.
All-inclusive couples resort, on the beach near
Castries, with access to restaurants and facilities
of two other Sandals properties on St. Lucia.

RESTAURANTS

Captain's Cellar Pub, + 1 758 450 0918.
Stone-walled cellar of historic fortifications
in Pigeon Point National Park, especially for
lunch and snacks.

Coal Pot, + 1 758 452 5566,
Caribbean ingredients and French-style cooking,
at the water's edge in Vigie Marina in Castries.

Courthouse Restaurant.
Seafood lunches next to the dock in Soufrière.

Dasheene, + 1 758 459 7323.
Haute Caribbean cuisine at Ladera Resort,
with a breathtaking view of the Pitons.

St. Martin/Sint Maarten 53

For more information: Saint-Martin Office du
Tourisme, Port de Marigot, 97150, Marigot,
Saint-Martin, + 590 590 87 57 21,
www.frenchcaribbean.com. Sint Maarten Tourist
Bureau, Vineyard Office Park, WB Buncamper Road
#33, Sint Maarten, Netherlands Antilles,
+ 599 542 2337, www.st-maarten.com.

HOTELS

Caravanserai Beach Resort, + 599 545 4000,
www.caravan-sxm.com.
Comfortable 70-room hotel at Maho Bay
(Dutch side).

La Samanna, + 590 590 87 6400,
www.lasamanna.com.
Luxurious villa resort on secluded Baie Longue
(French side).

Le Meridien L'Habitation, + 590 590 87 67 19,
www.lemeridien-hotels.com.
Upscale resort with its own beach at Anse Marcel
(French side).

Maho Beach Resort and Casino, + 599 545 2115,
www.mahobeach.com.
Extensive resort complex with several restaurants,
theatre and casino at Maho Bay (Dutch side).

Mary's Boon Beach Plantation, + 599 545 7000,
www.marysboon.com.
Friendly small hotel, next to the airport, on the beach
at Simpson Bay (Dutch side).

Pasanggrahan Royal Guest House, + 599 542 3588.
Historic 30-room hotel in the heart of Philipsburg
(Dutch side).

RESTAURANTS

Bistrot Caraibes, + 590 590 29 08 29.
Fresh fish and Creole specialities in Grand Case
(French side).

Bistrot Nu, + 590 590 87 97 09.
Traditional brasserie in Marigot (French side).

Enoch's Place, + 590 590 29 29 88.
Local dishes in a corner of the Marigot market
(French side).

Hot Tomatoes, + 599 545 2223.
Relaxed café with an eclectic Caribbean menu in
Simpson Bay (Dutch Side).

Le Tastevin, + 590 590 87 55 45.
Elegant multicourse French menu with wine pairings
in Grand Case (French side).

Terre de Haut 101

For more information: Office Municipal du Tourisme
des Saintes, 39, Rue de la Grande Anse, 97137
Terre de Haut, Les Saintes, Guadeloupe, F.W.I.,
+ 590 590 99 58 60, www.omt-lessaintes.com
and www.frenchcaribbean.com

HOTELS

Auberge Les Petits Saints, + 590 590 99 50 99,
www.petitssaints.com.
Antique- and art-filled 10-room hotel on a hillside
overlooking town.

Chez Tonton Fernand, + 590 590 99 56 73.
Two comfortable suites in a garden villa.

Hôtel Le Bois Joli, + 590 590 99 50 38,
www.hotel.boisjoli.com.
Thirty rooms and bungalows on two palm-lined
beaches near Pain du Sucre.

Hôtel Kanaoa, + 590 590 99 51 36,
www.kanaoa.com.
Pleasant balconied rooms at the edge of town.

RESTAURANTS

Auberge Les Petits Saints, + 590 590 99 50 99.
Gourmet dinners in an atmospheric hotel.

Coconuts Bar, + 590 590 99 53 02.
Informal bar and lively local watering hole.

Hôtel Le Bois Joli, + 590 590 99 50 38.
Elegant French and island cuisine overlooking
the water near Pain du Sucre.

La Paillote, + 590 590 99 50 77.
Fish and Creole specialities on the beach
at Marigot.

La Saladerie, + 590 590 99 53 43.
Fresh fish and light meals in a water-side,
art-filled setting.

Le Mambo, + 590 590 99 56 18.
Pizza and Creole dishes in a pavement café.

Sole Mio, + 590 590 99 56 46.
Fish and Italian cuisine overlooking the water.

Ti Kaz La, + 590 590 99 57 63.
Island cuisine in an open-air, waterside restaurant.

À La Belle Étoile (Terre de Bas), + 590 590 99 83 69.
Lobster and fresh fish on the beach a short walk
from the ferry dock.

Tobago 115

For more information: Tourism and Industrial
Development Company, P.O. Box 222, Maritime
Centre, 29 Tenth Ave., Barataria, Trinidad,
+ 1 868 675 7034, www.visittnt.com

HOTELS

Blue Haven Hotel, + 1 868 660 7400,
www.bluehavenhotel.com.
Stylish boutique hotel on Bacolet Bay.

Coco Reef Resort, + 1 868 639 8571,
www.cocoreef.com.
Upscale, Mediterranean-Caribbean-style resort
on the beach, near the airport.

Half Blue Moon Hotel, + 1 868 639 3551,
www.halfmoonblue.com.
Intimate, brightly decorated hotel on a hillside
above Bacolet Bay.

Le Grand Courlan Spa Resort, + 1 868 639 9667,
www.legrandcourlan-resort.com.
All-inclusive resort, with extensive spa facilities,
on Stonehaven Bay.

The Palms Villa Resort, + 1 868 635 1010,
www.thepalmstobago.com.
Six luxury three-bedroom plantation-style
villas, each with its own pool, on a 10-acre
estate near Scarborough.

Plantation Beach Villas, + 1 868 639 0455,
www.plantationbeachvillas.com.
Six two-storey villas, with a pool and restaurant,
on Stonehaven Bay.

RESTAURANTS

Café Coco, + 1 868 639 0996.
Spacious Mediterranean-style restaurant with
an extensive menu.

Golden Star, + 1 868 639 0873.
Local specialities, with steel-pan music and
talent shows.

Indigo, + 1 868 639 9635.
Seafood and local cuisine in a garden near
Stonehaven Bay.

Jemma's Sea View, + 1 868 660 4066.
Fish, chicken or shrimp with local side dishes
in a tree-house setting in Speyside.

Kariwak Village, + 1 868 639 8442.
Island specialities in a thatched-roof pavilion,
with music in the evening.

Turks & Caicos Islands 149

For more information: Turks & Caicos Islands
Tourist Board, P.O. Box 128, Front Street,
Grand Turk, Turks & Caicos Islands, B.W.I,
+ 1 649 946 2321; and Stubbs Diamond Plaza,
Providenciales, Turks & Caicos Islands, B.W.I,
+ 1 649 946 4970, www.turksandcaicostourism.com

HOTELS (GRAND TURK)

The Arches, + 1 649 946 2941,
www.grandturkarches.com.
Four two-bedroom apartments with good views
at the north end of Grand Turk.

Osprey Beach Hotel, + 1 649 946 2666,
www.ospreybeachhotel.com.
Comfortable 30-room beach-side hotel in
Cockburn Town.

Salt Raker Inn, + 1 649 946 2260,
www.saltraker.com.
Cosy 10-room inn in a nineteenth-century house
surrounded by a lush garden.

Parrot Cay Resort, + 1 649 946 7788,
www.parrot-cay.com.
Sixty deluxe rooms and villas, including an elegant,
Asian-style spa, on a private island.

HOTELS (PROVIDENCIALES)

Beaches, + 1 649 946 8000,
www.beaches.com.
All-inclusive family megaresort, part of the
Sandals chain.

Grace Bay Club, + 1 649 946 5050,
www.gracebayclub.com.
Ultra-luxurious Mediterranean-style beach hotel.

Ocean Club, + 1 649 946 5880,
www.oceanclubresorts.com.
Pleasant condominium resort on Grace Bay.

Sibonne, + 1 649 946 5547,
www.sibonne.com.
Brightly decorated motel-style resort on the beach.

RESTAURANTS (GRAND TURK)

Water's Edge, + 1 649 946 1680.
Seafood specialities overlooking the water.

Sandbar. Beach bar and restaurant on the beach
in Cockburn Town.

RESTAURANTS (PROVIDENCIALES)

Anacaona, + 1 649 946 5050.
Elegant gourmet water-view restaurant at the
Grace Bay Club.

Aqua Bar and Terrace, + 1 649 946 4763.
Casual cuisine at the Turtle Cove Marina.

Barefoot Café, + 1 649 946 5282.
Informal eatery with local seafood at Ports
of Call village.

Coco Bistro, + 1 649 946 5369.
Pasta and seafood in a colourful cottage setting.

Gilleys at Leeward, + 1 649 946 5094.
Seafood bar overlooking the Leeward Marina.

Smokey's on the Bay, + 1 649 9414463.
Local dishes and superb seafood in Blue Hills.

Virgin Gorda 157

For more information: British Virgin Islands Tourist
Board, P.O. Box 134, Road Town, Tortola, BVI, + 1 284
494 3134, www.bvitouristboard.com.

HOTELS

Biras Creek Resort, + 1 284 494 3555,
www.biras.com.
Luxury cottages on a scenic North Sound peninsula,
accessible only by launch.

Bitter End Yacht Club, + 1 284 494 2745,
www.beyc.com.
Hillside rooms in a water-sports-oriented resort
at North Sound.

Guavaberry Spring Bay Vacation Homes,
+ 1 284 495 5227, www.guavaberryspringbay.com.
One- and two-bedroom cottages with a private
beach near the Baths.

Leverick Bay Resort, + 1 284 495 7421,
www.VirginGordaBVI.com.
Hotel rooms, condominiums and luxury villas
around a marina.

Little Dix Bay Hotel, + 1 284 495 5555,
www.littledixbay.com.
Long-established luxe resort on its own beach.

RESTAURANTS

Chez Bamboo, + 1 284 495 5752.
Seafood specialities, in Spanish Town.

Flying Iguana, + 1 284 495 5277.
Fish and West Indian dishes in an open-air restaurant
near the airport.

Mad Dog, + 1 284 495 5830.
Sandwiches and sunset drinks on the road to the
Baths.

Mine Shaft Café, + 1 284 495 5260.
Lively café with a good sunset view.

Rock Café, + 1 284 495 5482.
Seafood restaurant with an atmospheric garden that
includes a waterfall among giant boulders.

Top of the Baths, + 1 284 495 5497.
Island dishes and seafood in an open-air restaurant
with a sunset panorama.

ACKNOWLEDGMENTS

ANTIGUA
Carlisle Bay Antigua
Curtain Bluff Resort

BAHAMAS
Bahamas Ministry of Tourism
Bluff House Beach Hotel
Dunmore Beach Hotel
Pink Sands
Sugar Apple Bed and Breakfast
Unique Village
Brendal's Dive Shop
Bahamasair

BARBADOS
Barbados Tourism Authority
Almond Beach Club & Spa

BONAIRE
Tourism Corporation Bonaire
Harbour Village Beach Club
Bonaire Exel

CURACAO
Curacao Tourist Board
Hotel Kura Hulanda

DOMINICA
National Development Corporation
Garraway's Hotel
Habitation Chabert
Sutton Place Hotel
Ken's Hinterland Adventure Tours & Taxi Service

DOMINICAN REPUBLIC
Casa Colonial Beach & Spa

GRENADA
Grenada Board of Tourism
True Blue Bay Resort
Mandoo Tours

GRENADINES
St. Vincent and the Grenadines Tourist Office
Creole Garden Hotel
Frangipani Hotel
Cotton House Resort
The Mustique Company

JAMAICA
Island Outpost
Goldeneye
The Caves

MARTINIQUE
Martinique Promotion Bureau/CMT USA
Comité Martiniquais du Tourisme
Cap Est Lagoon Resort and Spa
Sofitel Bakoua Coralia

NEVIS
Nevis Tourism Authority
Montpelier Plantation Inn

PUERTO RICO
The Horned Dorset Primavera

SABA
Saba Tourist Bureau
Ecolodge Rendez-Vous
Juliana's Hotel
Scout's Place
Winair

ST. BARTHÉLEMY
Hotel Guanahani

ST. JOHN
United States Virgin Islands Department of Tourism
Great Caribbean Getaways

ST. KITTS
St. Kitts Tourism Authority
Ocean Terrace Inn

ST. LUCIA
St. Lucia Tourist Board
Anse Chastanet Resort
Sandals
Air Jamaica

ST. MARTIN/ST. MAARTEN
St. Maarten Tourist Bureau
Mary's Boon Beach Plantation

TERRE DE HAUT
Office Municipal du Tourisme, Terre-de-Haut
Les Iles de Guadeloupe Comité du Tourisme
Auberge Les Petits Saints
Air Caraïbes

TOBAGO
Tourism and Industrial Development Company of Trinidad &
Tobago
Le Grand Courlan Spa Resort
The Palms Villa Resort
Tobago Express

TURKS & CAICOS ISLANDS
Turks & Caicos Tourist Board
Grace Bay Club
Osprey Beach Hotel
Parrot Cay Resort
Big Blue Unlimited
TCI SkyKing

VIRGIN GORDA
British Virgin Islands Tourist Board
Guavaberry Spring Bay Vacation Homes
Leverick Bay Resort

Thank you also to the following people and firms for their
assistance in connection with research for this book:

Adams Public Relations; Alice Marshall Public Relations;
American Airlines; Blue Sky Public Relations; Brandman
Public Relations; BWR Public Relations; Centric
Communications; Cheryl Andrews Marketing; Clare
Bradshaw Public Relations; Dennis Carlton; Gary Shillingford;
Jackie Cavet; Jackie Lewis; Laura Davidson Public Relations;
Lou Hammond & Associates; Martha Morano Public
Relations; Martin Public Relations; MDP Publicity Associates;
Melaine Communications; Nancy J. Friedman Public
Relations; Richartz Fliss Clark & Pope; Spectacular Ink Public
Relations; Spring, O'Brien & Company; Weber Shandwick
Worldwide.

Photography credit: Rip Bucks, p. 139.

travellers' guide